Also by Norma Cole

Books & Chapbooks

More Facts (Tente Press)
14000 Facts (a+bend press)
If I'm Asleep (Mermaid Tenement Press)
Where Shadows Will: Selected Poems 1988–2008 (City Lights Books)
Natural Light (Libellum Press)
Collective Memory (Granary Press)
At All (Tom Raworth & His Collages) (Hooke Press)
Do the Monkey (Zasterle Press)
a little a & a (Seeing Eye Books)
Burns (Belladonna Books)
Spinoza in Her Youth (Omnidawn)
Stay Songs, for Stanley Whitney (Bill Maynes Gallery)
The Vulgar Tongue (a+bend press)
Spinoza in Her Youth (A.Bacus)
Desire & its Double (Instress)
Quotable Gestures (CREAPHIS/un bureau sur l'Atlantique)
Mars (CREAPHIS/un bureau sur l'Atlantique)
Capture des lettres et vies du Joker (Format américain/un bureau sur l'Atlantique)
Contrafact (Potes & Poets Press)
Moira (O Books)
Mars (Listening Chamber Editions)
My Bird Book (Littoral Press)
Mon Livre des oiseaux (Foundation Royaumont)
Metamorphopsia (Potes & Poets Press)
Mace Hill Remap (Moving Letters Press)

Translations (Selected)

The Spirit God and the Properties of Nitrogen, Fouad Gabriel Naffah (Post-Apollo Press)
Notebooks, Danielle Collobert (Litmus Press)
Distant Noise, Jean Frémon. With Lydia Davis, Serge Gavronsky, Cole Swenson
(Avec Books)
Nude, Anne Portugal (Kelsey Street Press)
Crosscut Universe: Writing on Writing from France (Burning Deck Books)
A Discursive Space: Interviews with Jean Daive (Duration Press)
The Surrealists Look at Art: Essays by Aragon, Breton, Eluard, Soupault, Tzara.
With Michael Palmer (Lapis Press)
It Then, Danielle Collobert (O Books)

Other

SCOUT. Text/image work in CD ROM format (Krupskaya Press)
Catasters Broadside. Collaboration with Jess (Morning Star Editions)

TO BE AT MUSIC
Essays & Talks

TO BE AT MUSIC
Essays & Talks

Norma Cole

OMNIDAWN PUBLISHING

RICHMOND, CALIFORNIA

2010

Cover Art by Stanley Whitney
R & B, 2007
Oil on linen, 60 x 60 inches
Courtesy of Stanley Whitney and Team Gallery

Offset printed in the United States on archival, acid-free recycled paper
by Thomson-Shore, Inc., Dexter, Michigan

green
press
INITIATIVE

Omnidawn Publishing is committed to preserving ancient
forests and natural resources. We elected to print this title on
30% postconsumer recycled paper, processed chlorine-free. As
a result, for this printing, we have saved:

3 Trees (40' tall and 6-8" diameter)
1,169 Gallons of Wastewater
1 million BTUs of Total Energy
71 Pounds of Solid Waste
243 Pounds of Greenhouse Gases

Omnidawn Publishing made this paper choice because our
printer, Thomson-Shore, Inc., is a member of Green Press
Initiative, a nonprofit program dedicated to supporting authors,
publishers, and suppliers in their efforts to reduce their use of
fiber obtained from endangered forests.

For more information, visit www.greenpressinitiative.org

Environmental impact estimates were made using the Environmental Defense
Paper Calculator. For more information visit: www.edf.org/papercalculator

Library of Congress Catalog-in-Publication Data

Cole, Norma.
  To be at music : essays & talks / Norma Cole.
    p. cm.
  ISBN 978-1-890650-44-5 (pbk. : alk. paper)
  I. Title.
  PR9199.3.C585T6 2010
  814'.54--dc22
                                                2010026857

Published by Omnidawn Publishing, Richmond, California
www.omnidawn.com   (510) 237-5472   (800) 792-4957
          10 9 8 7 6 5 4 3 2 1
          ISBN: 978-1-890650-44-5

Acknowledgements

My heartfelt thanks to the poets and artists, curators and editors who occasioned these essays & talks.

"The Poetics of Vertigo," Oppen Lecture, December 3, 1998, Unitarian Center, San Francisco, published in the *Denver Quarterly*, Volume 34, No. 4, Winter 2000

"Start Singing," "Writing into the Twenty-First Century," *San Francisco State University Review* Benefit, San Francisco, November 30, 1994, published in the *San Francisco State University Review*, Volume 1, No. 2, 1995

"For Lorine Niedecker," *Conjunctions: 29, Tributes*, Fall 1997

"Giving Up the Private Property of the Self, or the Alienation Effect in Poets' Theater," New Langton Arts, San Francisco, February 2, 2002

"Goldie & Ruby: A Piece of Short Sets," Modernist Studies Association, Rice University, October 15, 2001

"of theory / of possibility," Women / Writing / Theory, *Raddle Moon* No. 11, 1992

"Untitled (M)," *The Grand Permission: New Writings on Poetics and Motherhood*, Eds. Brenda Hillman & Patricia Dienstfrey, Wesleyan University Press, 2003

"Nines and Tens: A Talk on Translation, "Kootenay School of Writing, Vancouver, 1991, Published in *Raddle Moon* No. 11, 1992

"In the Time of Prosody," Introductory Remarks, Browning Society, San Francisco, February 4, 1994

"A Minimum of Matter," *Even on Sunday: Essays and Archival Materials on the Poetry and Poetics of Robin Blaser,* Ed. Miriam Nichols, National Poetry Foundation, 2002

"Error of Locating Events in Time: for Edmond Jabès," *Apex of the M,* No. 1, Spring 1994

"A Few Words about Mina Loy," *Mina Loy: Woman and Poet,* Eds Maeera Schreiber & Keith Tuma, National Poetry Foundation, 1998

"A Picture Book without Pictures," *Crayon*, Issue 3, 2001

"(no longer or not yet) Translation and the Recovery of the Public World," Recovery of the Public World: Conference Honoring Robin Blaser, Vancouver, January 1995, published in *Recovery of the Public World: Essays on Poetics in Honor of Robin Blaser*, Eds. Ted Byrne & Charles Watts, Talonbooks, 1999

"Singularities: The Paintings of Stanley Whitney," Exhibition Essay, University of Dayton, 1991

"Ten Minutes to Talk about Experimental Writing: A Documentary," Naropa University, July, 1995, published in *Quarter After Eight*, 1999

"If It Were Christa Wolf," *Sulfur* 34, Spring 1994

"Yellow and...", "Introducing Marjorie Welish," Slought Foundation at the University of Pennsylvania, April 5, 2002, published in *Of The Diagram: The Work of Marjorie Welish*, Slought Books 2003

"Why I Am Not a Translator—Take 2," The Association of Writers & Writing Programs, Atlanta, March, 2007, published in the *Denver Quarterly*, Volume 41, No. 4, 2007

"At All—Tom Raworth and His Collages," Raworth Day, Notre Dame University, September 20, 2005, published as a chapbook by Hooke Press 2006

"Forever Amber," *A Broken Thing: Poets on the Line*, Eds. Emily Rosko & Anton Vander Zee, forthcoming from University of Iowa Press, 2011

Contents

TO BE AT MUSIC
Essays & Talks

THE POETICS OF VERTIGO

In Memory of Charles Watts

Sometime during the Fourth of July weekend I had a dream that I was looking at an open book. It was by George Oppen, and it was called *Posterity*. I had been thinking about legacy and reading *King Lear*. I had thought, suddenly, Is George Oppen Cordelia?

More specifically, I had been thinking about the limits he set for himself, for writing, the limits a writer sets and struggles with and against and sometimes through. These limits, once articulated, might provide clues about where the writer's ability to engage with other work...leaves off. That is, the limits of one's writing are the limits of one's reading.

These permeable and elusive limits, their negotiation as orientation, will be the recurrent points of reference of tonight's talk. Which does not eliminate further consideration of George, Cordelia and posterity.

This talk falls into four sections, the first of which will concern the introduction of terms. The second is called "The Preparation of Titles," a title itself taken or borrowed from a book of that name by French poet Joseph Guglielmi. The third addresses George Oppen and his work, attempting to map or remap some edges, and the fourth moves outwards from the blurred, tattered, fragmented or of necessity incomplete mapping of said edges.

I. "Illogical judgments lead to new experience." Sol LeWitt

Some *terms*:

The law of Terra inviolata which, in ancient times, protected the vulnerability of the earth seemed to forbid cutting through isthmuses or building artificial harbors, forbid, "in other words, radical alterations of the relationship between land and sea...." (Hans Blumenberg) This prohibition, or taboo, is reminiscent of that other one about building a tower into the heavens, the project everyone worked on as long as they understood each other.

The said. Experience as the said, coming to that.
Infancy, from in/fans, unable to speak, having experience before being able to speak. "...language appears as the place where experience must become truth." (Agamben)

Phone, a sound of spoken language, and the memory/phonology relationship. Writing and the body. Experience again. Body. Gesture. Not the "heroic" gesture, not heroic.
"As the philosophers say, linguistic activity takes place without self-knowledge." (Roman Jakobson)

Word. The word itself has been described as having "a halo, a nimbus, a glory, spheres of radiance, in other words a horizon called definition." (Maurice Natanson)

"The limits of my language mean the limits of my world." (Wittgenstein)
Limit is safety. It can also be a scandal, from the Greek *skandalon,* snare for an enemy, cause of moral stumbling, stumbling block, a trap.

So we are lost right from the start.

Vertigo: a common violation of the inner ear. A temporary environment. *Vertigo*: a turning around. The sensation of moving around in space (subjective vertigo) or having objects move about the person (objective vertigo). This is true vertigo and is a result of a disturbance of the equilibrium. Equilibrium is sometimes disturbed by an excess of light.

When pilots flew by sight, losing the horizon often meant plummeting straight down.

Horizon, high-water mark, threshold, orientation, the limit defining the furthest reaches….

And there is a second horizon, drawn from the site of subjectivity outwards, away. Because it is drawn out from one self, that one self sees it as a point, a blind spot, a stumbling block.

By definition, the horizon is that thing that we can almost or barely perceive, that recedes as we approach. This is movement and indicates that we are alive. Or is it simply a function of the round earth, a physical given responsible for virtual motion?

"*horizon or fringe* (Horizont; Hof in the sense of "halo"): the fringe of marginal acts and contents which surrounds the thematic core of the field of intentional consciousness." (Spiegelberg, 718)

When philosopher Husserl introduces this term into his work in an article published in 1894, he credits the term 'fringe' to William James who wrote about it in his essay, "The Stream of Thought." *Universals* are on the margin or fringe of individual conceptions deriving from experience.

The Husserlian idea of horizon or fringe provides a context or frame of reference "without which any account of even a single perception would be incomplete." (Natanson)

A little progression in time and space: for Husserl, exploration of experience is spatial, for Heidegger temporal, for Merleau-Ponty spatiotemporal.

Since Husserl, phenomenology has effectively used the term 'field of presence' to define the ambient space qualified by the spatiotemporal experience of perception. "Perception," wrote Merleau-Ponty, "provides me with a 'field of presence' in a broad sense, extending in two dimensions: the here-there dimension and the past-present-future dimension." (Chevrier, 157)

The halo or fringe or margin or horizon becomes, in the work of philosopher Aron Gurwitsch, a *zone* or *field*, a field of deregulation.

So the radio news report which states "Pakistan is not a source of trouble for Israel, it is beyond the Israeli horizon" can be experienced spatiotemporally as statement of a limit-experience or trouble-horizon.

"I choose to remain on this limit, on this line where something ends." (Jean-Luc Nancy) On the strand, at the edge of a field. Horizon was the working title for George Oppen's book *Seascape: Needle's Eye*.

Edge: The line that connects the dots. By a *graph*, mathematicians mean any group of points (called "vertices") connected by lines (called "edges"). So a triangle, for example, is a graph with three vertices and three edges. A poem is a navigational chart of moving edges.

The edge, according to Maurice Blanchot, in "La solitude essentielle," is the writer's risk, his orientation towards the "open violence of the work," which he also refers to as the horizon of an other force or power ("l'horizon d'un puissance autre").

Address is specific, a confidence. It appears to assume orientation, map, zip code. Paul Celan's "letter in a bottle" is an address, epitome of the dialogic. But perhaps this attempt at echolocation is a means rather than the end it seems, an act permitting access to a nexus we could call Key Signature plus Time Signature, the harmonics and tonalities of vulnerability and openness.

                                                          10.ix.98

Dear Charles,

According to neuroscientist Michael Gazzaniga, we have a spin doctor in our left brain. "We see connections where there are none."

Having lost the horizon, what happens to gravity? Do we understand Jean-Luc Nancy's title *The Gravity of Thought* literally? "What I am attempting to 'signify' here is nothing more than this: meaning at the limit of signification…." (Nancy, vii)

Dear Charles, During the period of time leading up to this evening, I encountered many possible points of entry into the materials….

Charles, what if the development of this talk continues through a series of so-called titles or *epic* titles (from *epos*, unwritten song sets, precursors to the written narrative). That would address my own obsession with illuminating or at least interrogating the relationship *title* and *text*, with its implicit hierarchical and conservative structure, a controlling structure which also stipulates *thesis* as conventional recognizable statement.

And what boundaries would be set in place by that decision, the decision to go with this approximate *durch-composiert* (*through-composed*) method invoking successive titles, their capitols, their body parts?

Idea, look, semblance, form, configuration, species, kind, class, sort, nature, a general or ideal form, type, model. Its Greek root *id-* is from *idein* which means to see. Idea, active form, is a constellation in which phenomena are composed in a gesture. Exposed. Activity is seen, registers at edges, moving out of frame.

"Ideas are the texture of experience…." (Merleau-Ponty)

Motion, Time, Measure: "And so time is regarded as the rotation of the sphere, in as much as all other ideas of motion are measured by it…."
(Aristotle)
Propose a development which is progression but not progress. Suppose in this case development without positive or negative value, merely change, movement, for example the movement of waves, motion which is time and refers beyond itself. Meaning is in the *rhythm* or *cadence*.

Improvisation: "Mere exposure to stimuli is enough to create preferences." (Joseph Ledoux) Already there is an orientation.

Improvisation and progression are development, orienting each other. Development, which is motion, is involved with preference. Preference is involved with subjectivity and direction and creates expectation. Writing is involved with movement, development, subjectivity, preference and direction. Subjectivity, which does not depend on pronouns, occurs in movement, development, writing and preference.

Improvisation and progression, their motion, include rupture, discontinuity. Discontinuity is startling, shatters expectation. The questions become how great a surprise can you tolerate and how small a surprise can you register? Linkages, not always lineages, like lists and like submerged autonomic systems, have direction.

Exile: "Esse est percipi," wrote Bishop Berkeley, being is being seen, being "known." Ovid wrote the *Tristia* from his experience beyond the pale, beyond the horizon of his known world. Far from his language context, far from his companions, his witnesses, the "outside-of-Rome" was mere space he could not recognize and value as place. Mandelstam, from his free fall of seering anticipation, wrote his *Tristia*. Oppen, like Cordelia or like Bartleby, "preferred not to" and could not. Mexico was a space that for him never became place.

Considerations of exile dovetail with questions about what defines or binds a work as, say, "American," a continuing preoccupation since this country's revolutionary beginning. What locates a work, and what is lost in overlocation?
Emersonian-American self-reliance states, "To believe your own thought, to believe what is true for you in your private heart is true for all men,—that is genius. Speak your latest conviction, and it shall be the universal sense." (Emerson)

Another perspective enjoins, "To speak out beyond his or her historical confinement has been a repeated mission of the concerned artist...." (Max Kozloff, 239)

Abstraction: Absence of representation. On a sliding scale, like improvisation. Meaning is unhooked from reference and inheres to varying degrees in other elements of a work, such as relationship, scale, color or cadence. In the sixties abstraction was "...becoming progressively more dogmatic in demanding that one's work be non-associative, formalistic and coolly objective." (Meyer Schapiro)

Frank Lloyd Wright, looking at Solomon Guggenheim's collection of painting in preparation for designing the Guggenheim Museum, referred to the abstractions as "lessons in fingerpainting," and asked, "What do you call this stuff?"

Abstract, in Western culture, is often a contentious term synonymous with "I don't get it."
Kenneth Baker in the *SF Chronicle*, October 1998, reassures us in his exhibition review: "*Undercurrents and Overtones* at CCAC is a reminder that abstract painting has conquered the world." It is clearly still a cultural benchmark, limit-horizon of the familiar, something to accept or reject with indignation. The very word "abstract" has itself come to refer to something too far out, too unfamiliar, *unheimlich*, unacceptable for whatever reason.

The poem is an abstract space defined by its being.

Intuition, Anschauung, is Husserl's name for the mental act by which some intellectual or perceptual content is directly apprehended.

Intuition has no interest in serving a community, no interest in knowing its constituency. The point at which intuition meets boredom is the site of lack of interest. This is where other knowing may enter, the horizon or line of sight may alter, where assumptions that permit ordinary functioning may not be called for.

II. Preparation of Titles (*Préparation des Titres*, JG)

Being a short text in stanzas, made of titles, each one having presented itself
as "A Possible Title for This Talk." Each will be addressed eventually.

"Little Things You Say and Do" or
"Rave on & Tell Me"
"Will You Have Memory Again?" or
"All Hands on Deck"

"Turn the Book Ninety Degrees" or
"Prohibition"
"Resistance to Memory" or
"The Silence of the Book"

"To Make a Thing That Looked Like That" or
"The Anxiety of the Disappearing Object" or
"Conditions Are Out of Control" and
"Now the Public Good Begins Again"

or "Conflicts of Interest" or
"Where Does Subversion Begin?"
"No Linkage" or
"Living Rupture" or
"The Other City"
"The Camera Speaks" or
"Authorship of the Reader"

"Six Lights and a Vacuum Cleaner" or
"A Confusing Question about a Need for Univocal Images Over Which
I Must Have Complete Control" or
"Living Bricolage" or
"Prematurely Nomadologist"

"From An Adjacent Booth" or
"Time's Signature"
"The Painted Veil of Reason" or
"Graph Paper" or
"Local Climate" or

"A Cloudburst on the Corner"

or "I Want to Live Outside Those Dates"
or "Linda Grew Up"
"The Application" or
"Every Event is Incredible"
"Hey Sailor!"

"The Philosopher's Surplus" or
"How Do You Say?" or
"Fall On Your Face"
"Where Experience Ends" or
"Inattentional Blindness"
"The Kids R Us" or
"Apocalypse Now & Then"

"Ruthless Abstraction, Disjunction and the Paratactic Life"
or "The Theater of the Neutral I" or
"Beyond Recognition" or
"Surface Does Not Point" or
"With All Due Respect" or
"Interested Movement" or
"With, To, Against, For, From" or

"Perception's Indicators,"
"Conditions Must Be Met" or
"Groping As Experience"
"The Sound of It" or
"What's Important"

"Choice and the Limits of Choice" or
"Rock Bottom"
"Seeing Beyond Reason" or
"Direct Apprehension?"
"Unsafe at Any Speed" or
"When I'm Gone" or

"I Started Looking for That Song" or
"How Many Poets Fit on the Point of a Pen?" or

"Fuck the Hermeneutical Boondoggle"
"Outstanding Considerations,"
"Witness or Accomplice?"
"The Dayroom,"
"Reality, or Clues for Nothing" or

"Lost Causality, The Case of The"
"(Logic) or Wall" or
"Observations Are the Fact" or
"The Writer's Head is Flat"

"Syntactical Intrigue"
"Postmark Where to Begin"
"Of a Book" or
"How to Hold It" or
"The Consequence of Objects"

"Notions of Circumstance,"
"Conjunctions of Causality" or
"Attributions"
"The Limbs, Their Names" or
"Kaput!"

"Another Shadow Play Behind the House" or
"Tired of the Past, of Remembering" or
"The Beauty of Contingency" or
"I Am the Messenger You May Kill"

"Santa Suicide" or
"What They Tell You"
"Cordoned Off" or
"Late, and I Have Not" or

"What's For Memory?"
"Just a Word with You" or
"Things of Yours"
"Self-Evident" or
"Somewhere There's Musicality"

or "One Blind Spot Leads to Another"
or "Much Later"
or "The Forest in the Trees"
"We Were Afraid of That"
or "The Vengeance of Order"

"Brand X" or
"Shocked into Being" or
"The World According to the Dark" or
"Throwing Your Life Away" or
"Nothing So Resembles Virtue"

"Tailspin" or
"The Floodplains of Relief" or
"The Erasure"
"The Evidence" or
"Your Associations Are Not Mine" or

"Too Pointed, He Said" or
"No Motion But in Things' Potential" or
"Juggling is a Skill" or
"Being Has a Form" or
"The Eye in the Hand" or
"The Eye That Binds"

"Horizon of the Half-Life" or
"Sight's Infallibility" or
"To Hell With the Rest of Us" or
"The New Vatican,"
"At Arm's Length" or
"Normal Passion"

"As a Matter of What Course?"
"And Then It's A Different Time" or
"The Afterlife of Influence" or
"I'm Not Going There" or

"I Can't Go There" or
"Elysian Fields" or

"By Candlelight" or
"What Grows There?" or
"When Speculation Turns to Dirt" or

"Do I Make Myself Plain?" or
"The Little I Wrote" or
"Walked in Fact"
"Indiscrete Series" or
"Because You Can't Go Back on the Texture of Experience"

or "Successive Incompletions"
or "Some Sustained"
or "The Suspensions of Capital"
or "Brushes the Surface"
or "What's Happening in the Left Hand Margin"
or "Towards Morning"
or "Private I, Tourist Eye"
or "The Understudy" or

"Mute Experience Ideas Scratch" or
"Moments Questions" or
"What the Missile Doesn't See" or
"Time Out Of My Mind" or
"My Mind Does It Not" or
"Scandal in Synecdoche" or
"Shift Happens" or
"Cunning Kenning" or
"The Close Moment" or
"The Infinite Rehearsal"

III. "Until you understand a writer's ignorance, presume yourself ignorant of his understanding,"

writes Robin Blaser, quoting Coleridge, in Blaser's splendid essay, "The Practice of Outside: For Jack Spicer."

George Oppen, in his essay, "The Mind's Own Place," claims the right to be in ignorance, to be in the dark, to find things out for himself, to blunder. He claims these rights for himself and for poets.

The essay itself was written on request, to be published in *The Nation*, but it was rejected on the grounds that it was not enough of an essay, the form was not recognizable enough in terms of the accepted model. Oppen refused to change it, to make it explain. His choice was not to publish. The writing would discover and meet its own readership eventually.

Mary Douglas, in her book, *Thought Styles*, writes, "When a new private thought comes into being, it may have a chance to escape being embedded in a social situation. It will then likely pay for its originality by being forgotten." Injunctions against the asocial, often conflated with the private, go back to Moses and before, but the distinctions do not hold. Is imagination private? Is reading private?

In a letter, Oppen writes, regarding the rejection of his piece, "I was thinking that the bad old times of the hole and corner poet were over, etc. etc. I cannot set myself to write 'privately.' I must get a mimeograph or something of the sort…and use it as a means of production. Absurd to undertake to speak for the editors rather than myself." There is hell to pay for the asocial nature of this heuristic thinking and writing.

The title of the essay in question, or, rather, not in question, is "The Mind's Own Place." Whose place is that? Although Oppen says his hero is Blake, this title is taken from Milton, from *Paradise Lost*, Book I, from the mouth of Satan, who is talking strategy to his ally, Beelzebub. This is the speech where he says:

... Farewell, happy fields,
Where joy forever dwells! Hail, horrors! hail,
Infernal World! and thou, profoundest Hell,
Receive thy new possessor—one who brings
A mind not to be changed by place or time;
The mind is its own place, and in itself
Can make a Heaven of Hell, a Hell of Heaven.

(250-255)

The underlying implications of Oppen's essay, and his attitude toward it, are built upon the very "darkness visible" of his particular not knowing, and on the risk of finding out.

Oppen is willing at this point to break the laws, the taboos, of sociality, of political activism, of *terra inviolata*. The claim is for the right of free fall, the right to let go of the familiar, of the horizon of experience, to go beyond it. "We can only do so when, with whatever difficulty, with whatever sense of vertigo, we begin to speak for ourselves."

"It is thought that carries us into the absolutely new." And it is the form the writing takes that permits thought to move at all. The troubled limit-horizons of the new are givens in the poems:

"...What I've seen
Is all I've found: myself"
(*Collected Poems* 40, *The Materials*)

and

"The play begins with the world"
(*CP* 215, *Seascape*)

The first quote, from "Product," sounds surprisingly like Nietzsche's Zarathustra, in the chapter "On Turmoil," where, after the shipwreck, "overcome by disgust, he sought some consolation—himself." (Blumenberg, 19) An old piece of received wisdom says own no more than what you can carry when the ship goes down. Another suggests you be not disdainful of the plank that saved you.

The Oppens returned from Europe, from their prolonged stay in France, in the thirties, aghast at the rise of Hitler, in fear for their own lives. Upon their return to the United States, they were horrified at the political and economic situation and threw themselves into political work. When the United States entered the war, so did George Oppen. After the war, threatened by the rise of rabid McCarthyism, the Oppens fled to Mexico and lived a life of exile there, at times under surveillance, not really there, not anywhere.

It was a protracted period of survival, of survival and of principle. Later, when Oppen has returned to writing and has claimed the right to throw everything into question, he will move his questions, albeit uncomfortably, as his thought requires, that his thought and prosody move. That is, some questions must occur in order that others become visible on the horizon.

But during the period prior to this, the period when Oppen was not writing, "…there were some things I had to live through, some things I had to think my way through, some things I had to try out—and it was more than politics, really; it was the whole experience of working in factories, of having a child, and so on." (Dembo interview)

Oppen writes another, slightly different version of this explanation to his friend Julian Zimet, where the reference to the relationship between writing and family life, or more specifically, parental responsibility, is foregrounded:

"Julian: there were only some fifteen years that political loyalties prevented me from writing poetry. After that I had to wait for Linda to grow up. Yes: the poem says that I don't like to die. Poppa couldn't say it: Buddy (Oppen's nickname) says it. Go lean on someone else."

Go lean on someone else. Here is a glimpse of the fathomless crack between the biography and the life, between Poppa and Buddy/George Oppen/Poet. This split is related to the startling moment where Mallarmé inscribes a copy of the sumptuous limited edition of L'Après-midi d'un Faune ("The Afternoon of a Faun"), illustrated by Manet, to his young son Anatole:

"à 'tole,

"ne le déchire pas

"Stéphane Mallarmé"

"To 'tole, don't tear it, Stéphane Mallarmé." The intimate nickname, the paternal finger raised in warning, the formal signature of the poet, all on the same page. There will be a time in the future of both these parent/poets where these distinctions blur. For Mallarmé, this will occur after his son's death.

For George Oppen, there have been things he cannot imagine saying to his daughter. For instance, "Go lean on someone else." From a crossed-out paragraph, "Some ideas are not politically useful, or useful to the childhood of a daughter." (*Selected Letters* 66)

But the poem will not abide such restrictions. There is a statement of this law with which many of us are already familiar. This is where Jack Spicer says, in his first Vancouver Lecture, 1965: "Like if you want to say something about your beloved's eyebrows and the poem says the eyes should fall out, and you don't really want the eyes to fall out or have even any vague connection. Or you're trying to write a poem about Vietnam and you write a poem about skating in Vermont."

Curiously, in a letter from 1963, Oppen, responding to Gil Sorrentino, writes, "I haven't read Spicer but I will." Immediately following is a letter to Denise Levertov in which Oppen writes: "There are things we believe, or would like to believe, or think we believe, which 'will not substantiate themselves in the concrete materials of the poem.'" (*SL* 81)

The asocial radicality claimed by and for poetry is explicit in the work of Oppen's contemporary, Lorine Niedecker, who writes with trenchant clarity:

> My friend tree
> I sawed you down
> but I must attend
> an older friend

the sun
          (My Life By Water...)

Oppen continues in the Zimet letter: "A difficulty about poetry or
any such thing within a family is that one expects that one's father or
mother would say something clearer, more complete, closer to you than,
say, a puritan stranger like Emily Dickinson. Can't always. Proving
indirectly that conversation is not really an art." Conversation is bound
to and by the laws of the social. And this letter evidences a discourse of
binding responsibility struggling with its bindings.

These bindings alert us to the restricted and literal conception
of address which had been operative for Oppen. There were two
categories Oppen articulated, "the ones I love," for whom he says he
writes, and "the enemy." In poetry, this must shift, and it will in time.
But in 1958, Oppen cites something his daughter Linda had written
to him, from "away," from college: "You'd write very differently if you
wrote poems now."

Linda, the scout, the advance-guard, has moved back to the United
States before her parents' return, a return which will be less a "moving
back" than they know. Oppen sends her his new poems, commenting:
"I send proof that it's not altogether so (somewhat to my horror)."

He writes to Linda in intimate ease, and as though she is Mnemosyne,
Memory herself. "We were making a space around ourselves...," he
explains. In the telling, he is remaking a past, a past out of which they
can now live.

In 1958, the Oppen parents, having received permission to obtain their
American passports, prepare to move from Mexico back to the United
States, where President Eisenhower has charged that the Democratic
Party is dominated by radicals. Government security clearance checks,
then, as now, demand whether you have ever been a member of the
Communist Party and whether you are a homosexual.

In 1958, the first domestic jet airline passenger service has begun,
William Burroughs's *Junkie* has just been published, John Cage is
teaching at the New School, and a group show called *The New American*

Painting, which includes much Abstract Expressionist work, travels in Europe and will be shown the following year at the Museum of Modern Art in New York. Donald Allen's anthology, *The New American Poetry,* is in preparation and appears in 1960. The Objectivist poets are not in it.

Between the return in 1958 and the publication of "A Mind's Own Place" in 1963, George Oppen struggles with reorientation. The place has changed, the stumbling blocks are daunting. He must face himself, his blind spots, his own dark places.

"You would write differently," Linda has observed, coming into contact with the new. In the pressing need to change, Oppen has begun to face his own resistance as well as to envision a merging of the streams of "the grandson of the immigrant and the descendant of the puritan." It is not so surprising that in the post-WWII awareness of the awesome possibility of total global destruction, "a new form is incomprehensible."

> …From any window, the day
>
> Flawless and without exterior
> Without alternative. But to the tenant
>
> The future is all chance…
>   ("Tourist Eye," *CP* 44)

Troubled by what he articulates as his need to "loosen up," Oppen writes:

> The poems have too much point
> As tho I need invent
> The thing is in my mind always, available,
> Juggler, why need I invent so much
> Tho I think only of the coasts, figures of men and animals
> On the silent coasts.
>   ("The Phonemes," *Sulfur* 25, 35)

Moving, then, with the momentum of this need and with its apparatus of awkwardness, the "I know" or "I remember" as framing device begins to abstract itself incrementally, from the personal to the first person as a neutral space, a formal gesture which serves to introduce … uncertainty. Miming the known, it is the very stance of authority, setting propositions up for a fall.

> Endlessly, endlessly
> The definition of mortality
>
> The image of the engine
>
> That stops.
> We cannot live on that.
> I know that no one would live out
> Thirty years, fifty years if the world were ending
> With his life.
> The machine stares out,
> Stares out
> With all its eyes.
>
> (*CP* 19)

Ironically echoing the authority of Whitman's immortal "Out of the cradle endlessly rocking," this link provides in a split-second's recognition an archive, a history, a chart, a set of points, an edge against which to measure, or from which to push off for the new rhythm of experience, the new cadence which will be the new perishability.

In 1960, Oppen had written to Cid Corman, "I think of form as immediacy, as the possibility of being grasped or I look for the thinnest possible surface…. I am much more afraid of a solid mass of words." Oppen demands form that gives not "heightened emotion" but rather "graspability," a word for which he has apologized.

He has reached the limit of choice, and incurs a shattering in order to move. His shattering is quiet, occurring in small ways, in the different and new use of a pronoun, or a different negotiation with space, a new dynamics. A more than able seaman, he learns to navigate in the fog. The "I know" and "I remember" give out upon the abyss or into the unfathomable, into an imagination of the eventual dark, the dark Robert Duncan will describe as "this state/ that knows nor sleep nor waking, nor dream." And so we see a new metaphysical poetry forming.

"I think poetry has its own, different relation to knowing because …
you cannot define the object of the pursuit."
(Claude Royet-Journoud, *Lingo*)

Graspability is a form of intentionality. Although "the play must
begin with the world," the universe is expanding. Oppen's work will
continue to be a marquetry of reference and echo where in a brief space
the reader may encounter Goya, Shelley, Heidegger, the Bible, Blake,
Rimbaud, Reznikoff, Shakespeare, the old anonymous song forms.

"Whitman has been no use to me….I always feel that deluge and soup
of words is a screen for the uncertainty of his own identity." In "A
Mind's Own Place," Oppen credits Williams, "the most American of the
American poets of his generation," with having freed him from needing
Whitman. Whitman, however, remains a presence, quoted directly and
reverberating in what for Oppen is a new prosodic extension.

Oppen's "poetics of poverty" will find their "shape," their austerity, at
times lush, turbulent:

> The space a woman makes and fills
> After these years
> I write again
> Naturally about your face.
> (*CP* 53)

4+3+3+(4+3), an algebra of excess. Lines release syntactically,
semantically, rhythmically and romantically, establishing the geometry
"I" and "your face," remapping the written I onto the face and into the
ear of the other, their edge joining two points, referencing two beings,
binding or at least defining that abstract space, the relation between
emotion (not heightened, but motion) and cadence.

Oppen continues to negotiate between what he identifies as open-
ended form and excess. Disruptions are words joined paradoxically
by gaps where the poem enters. Inflected awareness is the material
playground, and what was experienced by Oppen as obfuscation or
abstraction begins to be read as a means to engender the uncertain space
of thought.

Oppen describes the internal dynamics of the line which for him must have "the sense of the whole line, not just its ending." On the other hand, his increasing sense of open-ness and of the potential of imagination place him on the verge of releasing sequence from logic, from causality, creating (and he has acknowledged that creation is violent) new space in the poem.

The potential of this uncoupling of sequence from causality will motivate much of the exploration and unbearable play of writers Oppen refers to as "the youngsters": sequence ignoring consequence, consequence becoming occurrence, exploding the horizon.

There are negotiations with form that have simply eluded Oppen. In 1949, painter Robert Motherwell observed, "One might say today that the morality of a picture is unusually dependent on what the artist refused to accept in it as bearable. Modern pictures—'abstract' ones, that is—tend to be the residues of a moral process." Oppen does not in principle object to abstraction but has stated emphatically that it bores him.

Yet boredom is not unwelcome. It might be a version of "the unbearable" Heideggerian "boredom," the space of potentiality to which Oppen, reading and rereading Heidegger's "What is Metaphysics?" was so attracted. This is the unoccupied zone or field into which may enter the activity of intuition, the "intuition of existence… intuition of things… independent of self… permanent…." (*SL* 88) In time, Oppen admits that he cannot achieve the poem of permanence, the work of "final affirmation," for "the ear rebels."

Oppen had written, "My hero is Blake, who did everything as simply and clearly as THAT THING could be done—Not Louis and his crabbedness," that "crabbedness" and the "imaginary geometry" for which Oppen expressed real disdain. He commented about *A* that Zukofsky's motor was running in neutral, and ridiculed the Catullus translations. Years later, upon rereading sections of *A*, he was surprised to find them "much more moving, and much simpler, than I had remembered."

There is an odd coaxial coincidence in the beginnings of two works by these two poets inextricably linked, at first in cooperation and then in rigorous contention.

From Oppen's book *This In Which*, the poem, "A Narrative," section 11, begins

> River of our substance
> Flowing
> With the rest. River of the substance
> Of the earth's curve, river of the substance
> Of the sunrise, river of silt, of erosion, flowing
> To no imaginable sea. But the mind rises
>
> Into happiness, rising
>
> Into what is there.
> > (*CP* 140)

And Zukofsky's *A*-11 begins

> River that must turn full after I stop dying
> Song, my song, raise grief to music
> Light as my loves' thought, the few sick
> So sick of wrangling: thus weeping,
> Sounds of light…
> > (*A* 124)

At moments they mirror each other, meeting in words, in song, in the nothing between the body and being washed away.

In 1975, puzzled by the reception of his *Myth of the Blaze* ("a remarkable silence"), Oppen writes to Duncan, "But I thought I was simply pointing to things."

IV. "Passaic seems full of holes...." Robert Smithson

Oppen's "crystal/ center of the rock" (*CP* 254) has led through Robert Smithson's Site/Non-Sites and Clark Coolidge's Smithsonian Depositions to Laura Moriarty's virtual site, "non," a poetry/poetics website.

A poem opens with the words "Dear Lexicon," a poem constructed as cascading serial address, whose penultimate stanza reads:

> Dear George, So long
> Will you now have memory again?
>   (Michael Palmer, "Baudelaire Series")

It could almost be a letter. But George and the poem have merged. A baffling temporal radiance is introduced in these apparently simple lines. The holes or memory gaps which were Oppen's fate become potentially the reader's in an act of reverse anticipation, in an injunction against forgetting, against forgetting Oppen, who had himself thought he was writing to his metonymy, "posterity—Linda."

In his series of "Songs for Sarah," Michael Palmer dissolves Oppen's temporal dilemma by absorbing it into the poem. The address to his daughter, "for when she's older," is released from biography into the abstract atemporal space of permission, permission to inhabit fully the imagination and the opening of the means of address.

In 1968 Clark Coolidge's *ING* appeared from Angel Hair Books. In it, he moves "from diction to words and their parts." This introduces a cadence where reading time is what Oppen might have called abstract time, each morpheme and phoneme demanding consideration on its own and then in relation to the elements around it, in the space around. This space and the elements in it, their unfamiliarity, demand that the reader rely on the fullest available complement of linguistic experience, privileging neither written nor oral. Musicality here is equally visual and auditory, these materials enhancing and extending each other in the service of a new economy inventing itself. Single notes. Notes in small clusters. Space of reverberation, space as compositional element, the space Miles Davis praises in Shirley Horne's singing: "the space I make in my work." (Horne, radio interview)

This unmaking (unmasking?) becomes a progression, an array of graspabilities. With its capitals, its parentheses, its numerals, salts and minerals, Coolidge plays the horizon of tension between the inchoate and the explicit. It is his instrument with which he quotes the elements of language as Robert Smithson quotes elements in the physical world, holes included.

Coolidge's interest in "syntax as axial armature" (*Polaroid*) is renewed after the period of *ING* and *Space* (1970). Parts of speech become the players and the action, "…a chain of adjectives disguised as stores…." (*Smithsonian Depositions*) in a kind of narrative that Oppen might identify as "narrative of nothing." For him, narrative, in its comforting predictability, was at an end, "since every life ends badly," in shipwreck.

But a new narrative, not merely a comfort narrative, might also have proven unacceptable. There is a delicate balance in improvisation where the music is not yet familiar and almost too far out to be heard. This point is always moving, a moving point in the dynamics of the work itself. It can be utterly disorienting.

Trying to fix his location, Oppen had once written: "The pop art—a Disneyland tour of Dadism? Or the anger, the destructiveness of the homosexual, the totally disconnected, the man without natural valences—to him not only the structure but the purposes of society must seem AT ALL MOMENTS totally absurd." (Quoted in Kevin Killian, "The Phantom of the Opera," *Argento Series*, Krupskaya Press 2001; in *George Oppen: Selected Prose, Daybooks, and Papers*, University of California Press 2007. Edited and with an introduction by Stephen Cope, p. 59.) Turning on an observation predicated upon an experience not his own, yet discovering commonality with it, Oppen struggled in the direction of apprehension.

Further on, he noted: "But for me the sense of thinking beyond what I already know ^or what someone already knows^ is terrifying." (Ibid, p. 78) And then, "of course they are even entitled to equality. They have a perfect right to go to hell with us since they want to… the art world has become the perfect duplication of the industrial concerns together with the money of the industrialists." An astonishment of constraints.

Life, biography, the confusion of self, provide endless "Bewilderment," the title of Fanny Howe's recent "talk" (Small Press Traffic 1998) in which she identified her writing strategies for attempting to slip beyond these constraints. The talk ends with a statement that "the point of art is to show that life is worth living by showing that it isn't." Which activates the notion of value itself, of worth.

> And then they all go back to their lives
> But I don't have a life. I have
> This inestimable work.
> > (Coolidge, "Paris")

"The poem may have to mean nothing for a while or reflect in its meaning just the image of meaning." (Bernadette Mayer, "The Obfuscated Poem") Abstraction is named by Mayer as one of her materials:

> Scatter the dictionaries, they don't
> Tell the truth, I mix up words with truth
> And abstraction with presence...
> > ("Mutual Aid")

This generation of drivers has rearranged the horizon, in order "to talk about everything important at once and get it generating further." (Coolidge, *Sulfur* 18) Yet in *Smithsonian Depositions*, he acknowledges "the conditions of an increasingly limited set."

But the conditions of limits are continuously being displaced by the mind's own made place of another work. Here are two passages from Bernadette Mayer's poem, "Eve of Easter":

> Milton, who made his illiterate daughters
> Read to him in five languages
> Till they heard the news he would marry again
> And said they would rather hear he was dead
> Milton who turns even Paradise Lost

Into an autobiography, I have three
Babies tonight, all three are sleeping:
Rachel the great great great granddaughter
Of Herman Melville is asleep on the bed
Sophia and Marie are sleeping
Sophia namesake of the wives
Of Lewis Freedson the scholar and Nathaniel Hawthorne
Marie my mother's oldest name, these three girls
Resting in the dark, I made the lucent dark
I stole images from Milton to cure opacous gloom
...

Eve of Easter, I've inherited this
Peaceful sleep of the children of men
Rachel, Sophia, Marie and again me
Bernadette, all heart I live, all head, all eye, all ear
I lost the prejudice of paradise
                              (The Golden Book of Words)

Oppen Lecture
December 3, 1998
Unitarian Center
San Francisco

Published in
Denver Quarterly
Volume 34, No. 4
Winter 2000

Selected Bibliography

Agamben, Giorgio. *Infancy and History: Essays on the Destruction of Experience*, trans. Liz Heron (London and New York: Verso 1993)

Blanchot, Maurice. "La solitude essentielle," *L'espace littéraire* (France: Gallimard 1955)

Blaser, Robin, "The Practice of Outside," *The Collected Books of Jack Spicer* (Santa Barbara: Black Sparrow Press 1980)

Blau DuPlessis, Rachel, ed., *Selected Letters of George Oppen* (Durham and London: Duke 1990)

Blumenberg, Hans, *Shipwreck With Spectator: Paradigm of a Metaphor for Existence*, trans. Steven Rendell (Cambridge, MA and London, England: MIT 1997)

Celan, Paul, "Speech on the Occasion of Receiving the Literature Prize of the Free Hanseatic City of Bremen," *Paul Celan: Collected Prose*, trans. Rosmarie Waldrop (UK: Carcanet 1986)

Chevrier, Jean-François, *The Year 1967 From Art Objects to Public Things Or Variations on the Conquest of Space* (Barcelona: Fundacio Antoni Tapies 1997)

Coolidge, Clark, *ING* (New York: Angel Hair Books 1968)
——————, "Listener's Reach," *Sulfur* 18 (Ypsilanti MI Winter 1987)
——————, "Paris," *o-blek* 4 (Stockbridge, MA Fall 1988)
——————, *Polaroid* (Berkeley & New York: Big Sky & Adventures in Poetry 1975)
——————, *Quartz Hearts* (San Francisco: THIS, 1978)
——————, *Smithsonian Depositions & Subject to a Film* (New York: Vehicle Editions 1980)
——————, *Space* (New York: Harper & Row 1970)

Cuddihy, Michael, ed., *George Oppen: A Special Issue* (*Ironwood* 5 1975)
——————, *George Oppen: A Special Issue* (*Ironwood* 26 1985)

De Salvo, Donna, with a contribution by David Moos, *Forces of the Fifties: Selections from the Albright-Knox Gallery* (exhibition catalogue), Wexner Center for the Arts, Ohio State University 1996

Dembo, L.S., "George Oppen" (interview conducted on 25 April 1968), *Contemporary Literature* 10 (Spring 1969)

Duncan, Robert, *Groundwork II: In the Dark* (New York: New Directions 1987)

Gadamer, Hans-Georg, *Gadamer on Celan: "Who Am I and Who Are You? and Other Essays*, trans. and edited by Richard Heinemann and Bruce Krajewski. With an Introduction by Gerald L. Bruns (Albany: State University of New York 1997)

Gazzaniga, Michael, *The Mind's Past* (Berkeley, Los Angeles, London: University of California Press 1998)

Guglielmi, Joseph, *La préparation des titres* (France: Flammarion 1980)

Gurwitsch, Aron, *Théorie du champ de la conscience* (Paris: Desclée de Brouwer, 1957)

Hatlen, Burton, ed., *George Oppen: Man and Poet* (Orono: National Poetry Foundation, University of Maine 1981)

Heidegger, Martin, "What is Metaphysics?" *Basic Writings* (New York: Harper & Row 1977)

Howe, Fanny, "Bewilderment" (Talk, Small Press Traffic, San Francisco, 1998)

Jakobson, Roman, *Six Lectures on Sound and Meaning*, trans. John Mepham (Cambridge, MA and London, England: MIT Press 1981)

Killian, Kevin, "The Phantom of the Opera," in *Poems for Matthew Shepard*, ed. Scott Gibson (New York: Painted Leaf Books 1999)

Kozloff, Max, "Gilles Peress and the Politics of Space," *Lone Visions, Crowded Frames: Essays On Photography* (Albuquerque: University of New Mexico Press 1994)

Ledoux, Joseph, *The Emotional Brain* (New York: Touchstone 1966)

Mayer, Bernadette, *A Bernadette Mayer Reader* (New York: New Directions 1992)
_____, *The Golden Book of Words* (New York: Angel Hair Books 1978)

Merleau-Ponty, Maurice, *Le visible et l'invisible* (France: Gallimard 1964)

Moriarty, Laura, *non* (http://socrates.berkeley.edu/~moriarty)

Nancy, Jean-Luc, *The Birth to Presence* (Stanford: Stanford University Press 1993)
_____, *The Gravity of Thought*, trans. François Raffoul & Gregory Recco (New Jersey: Humanities Press International, Inc. 1997)

Natanson, Maurice, *Edmund Husserl: Philosopher of Infinite Tasks* (Evanston: University of Chicago Press 1973)

Oppen, George, *Collected Poems* (New York: New Directions, 1975)
_____, "From *DAYBOOK ONE, DAYBOOK TWO,* and *DAYBOOK THREE*: A New Selection from George Oppen's Working Papers," prepared by Stephen Cope (unpublished)
_____, "Meaning Is to Be Here: A Selection from the Daybook," prepared by Cynthia Anderson (*Conjunctions* 10, 1987)
_____, *Primitive* (Santa Barbara: Black Sparrow Press 1979)
_____, "The Circumstances: A Selection From George Oppen's Uncollected Writing," Rachel Blau Duplessis, ed. (*Sulfur* 25, 1989)
_____, "The Mind's Own Place" (*Montemora* 1, 1975)
_____, *The Selected Letters of George Oppen* (Durham, N.C.: Duke University Press 1990)

Oppen, Mary, *Meaning: A Life* (Santa Barbara: Black Sparrow Press 1978)

Palmer, Michael, *Notes for Echo Lake* (San Francisco: North Point Press 1981)
_____, *Sun* (San Francisco: North Point Press 1988)

Schapiro, Meyer, "On Some Problems in the Semiotics of Visual Art: Field and Vehicle in Image-Signs," *Theory and Philosophy of Art: Style, Artist and Society. Selected Papers* (New York: George Braziller 1994)

Spiegelberg, Herbert, *The Phenomenological Movement: A Historical Introduction* (The Hague: Martinus Nijhoff 1960)

Tuan, Yi-Fu, *Space and Place: The Perspective of Experience* (Minneapolis: University of Minnesota Press 1977)

Zukofsky, Louis, *A 1-12* (Kyoto: Origin Press 1959)

START SINGING

in this account, confusion*
is a place

it's in my silence
          —Nostalgia

"leaving order as a way of starting over it's impossible to repeat" *(Mars)*

16.vii.94 This, the last line of "What Others Had Told Me," written
more than three years ago, wants, today, to be read "impossible to retreat."
Scrawled in my notebook on an airplane SFO-Paris, this entry is dated,
like everything in the notebooks. But, looking at it today, I realize
that I had actually written 16.vii.74. So much for keeping track of the
numbers of years.

To list possibilities and dismiss them is a way of elaborating or
describing a "negative poetics," the invisible woman walks through
the rain, everything seen through her, through rain and through her.
Would you be so kind as to look at my eyes, as to look at the points of
view behind false opposites. (At this point, I could have made an other
different shape, *but did not realize it.*) A form of greeting sent out from
a century. From captivity. From exile. Raise your glass in wordless toast.
Ashbery, from "The System": "The facts of history...the oral kind that
goes on in you...." Invention or lamentation, "separation is the first
fact," from *My Bird Book.* From Michael Palmer's *Sun,* "you are in //
me as history I fix / and crystal to it." Ashbery, "The System": "...the
progress toward infinity had crystallized in them...." In all specificity, are
words the image of thought? asked the gizmologist. Blast and dazzle.

Robert Walser, "There's something missing when I don't hear music,
and when I do, then there's really something missing."

---

* Philo of Alexandria, "Treatise on the Confusion of Languages"

From *My Bird Book*:
>   as it was now / to think in rhythm / in close attendance... //
>   ...measures loosely assembled...
>   ...thought claims scaffold in the fact...
>   ...A model of vigor sets up a measure...
>   ...In this sung desire images rub up against each other....

Nate Mackey, *Talisman* interview: "You know, in language we inherit the voices of the dead."

This is where theory tries to catch up with poetry.

"I feel cornflakes how they / are grown in a digital state."
(Nostalgia) All sounds are off, although experience isn't everything. The current obsession with guessing about "the millenium" reminds me of The Millenium Falcon, *Star Wars*, my son's childhood, his fantasy: "when the nuclear disaster occurs, we'll get into our spaceship and blast off the earth."

"When they were scared, I'd start singing." (Bosnian refugee, in Chris Marker's *Prime Time in the Camps*, Camp Rosni, 1993)

Working, I am always in a present moment which consists of and insists upon looking forwards and backwards at the same time. It is a vigilance, an attention, a careful listening, an effort, serious play. In this way, we are the future of poetry, the ones who are writing, those who are reading. How we attend to each other. The ongoing conversation, the small presses, the magazines, on paper or online. In the face of...

I'm interested in what we can know, or what we can ask, and how poetry is a form of this asking and knowing, this trying to remember or trying to foresee, or to grasp what is ungraspable, and play with it in a territory of risk, and of permission. Is it true that you can only long for something in the past, something gone? Every day, for each day, there are entries in this book (lifts her notebook), possibly made up of many separate notations, thoughts in relation to what I'm reading, the news, conversations, ongoing considerations, dialogue with an idea, a "concern," one of "my" concerns, a question I am keeping in mind or that is keeping me in mind. Each day begins with its written date.

In this way, it is additive, quantitative; and, since we are changed by our thoughts (thought as experience) and by the things we make and witness as they look back at us, witness us, we are apprehended by them and we are changed. The writing changes. And so what accumulates in this additive way changes qualitatively, irreversibly. And so I wonder, but very occasionally, what I'll experience when I write the date of the new century. In answer to your question is it a concern of mine, not particularly, no. There are so many days and nights between now and then. You see how literally I take everything? How my imagination is literal? This is one of my concerns. As is memory, and history in the word, and what happens, what is *made* when the words are placed by or near each other. As is memory and the representation of it, what it gives (gives way to), and how it shapes thought. How could language exist without memory? How does memory exist without language? "In quella parte del libro della mia memoria..." Dante, *La vita nuova* ("In that part of the book of my memory..." D.G. Rossetti tr.)

Insistent concerns, from *Mace Hill Remap*, "possibility," "resistance," "song," "time," "to eliminate security," "stripping discourse," "discrete and continuous," "will," "memory of probability," "truth is a widow," "Imaginations law hits frames," "spaces gather," "that tongue be time," "reckoning in a work of form ideas of time." From *Metamorphopsia*, "spell by binding," "Love replaces time," "place of missing parts," "say things / and hear the sound." From *Moira*, "more towards a multiple exposure," "but sometimes the emotional body," "the sense of time in a form," "the materiality of this music."

I'll conclude these preliminary remarks with words from Susan Gevirtz's *Prosthesis*: "in the gentle and long the impossible...."

"Writing into the Twenty-First Century"
SFSU Review Benefit
30 November, 1994
Published in *SFSU Review*
Volume, No.2 1995

FOR LORINE NIEDECKER

"Guido, I wish that Lapo, thou and I,
  Could be by spells conveyed, as it were now,
Upon a barque, with all the winds that blow...."
Dante to Cavalcanti, trans. Rossetti[1]

"Robin, it would be a great thing if you, me, and Jack Spicer
Were taken up in a sorcery with our mortal head so turnd...."
Robert Duncan, "Sonnet 3, *From Dante's Sixth Sonnet*"[2]

"I wish you and Louie and Celia and I could sit around a table. Otherwise,
poetry has to do it."
Lorine Niedecker, letter to Cid Corman, October 1964[3]

fly back to it each summer[4]

Tribute, from *tribuere*, to assign, give pay, eventually metaphorizes from
actual payment in acknowledgement of submission, or in exchange for
the promise of peace, to homage paid, or acknowledgement of esteem,
affection. Edmund Spenser's first line of the proem "*To His Booke*"
echoes Chaucer with affection and esteem:

"Goe little booke: thy selfe present"[5]
from
"Goe, litel bok, go litel myn tragedye,"[6]

Old words make new worlds, place is idea. Think of the forms water
takes: Spinoza, Burns, Xenophanes, Blake, Sappho, Dostoievsky, "the
James brothers," William Carlos Williams, the Webbs, Jefferson,

---

[1] *Dante and his Circle*, ed. & trans. Dante Gabriel Rossetti (London, 1874) 143.
[2] Robert Duncan, *Roots & Branches* (NY, 1964) 124.
[3] "*Between &Your House and Mine*": *The Letters of Lorine Niedecker to Cid Corman*, 1960 to 1970, ed. Lisa Pater Faranda (Durham, 1986) 48,
[4] Lorine Niedecker, *My Life By Water: Collected Poems 1968* (UK, 1970) 41. This line is cited in Norma Cole, *My Bird Book* (LA, 1991) 28.
[5] Edmund Spenser, *The Shepheardes Calender* (1579; in *Norton Anthology*, 1962) 530.
[6] Geoffrey Chaucer, *Troilus and Criseyde* (c.1380; NY, 1987) 1. 1786.

Pasternak, Engels, the Brontes, Dickinson, Ovid, Einstein, Pound, Gilbert White, Audubon, Duke Ellington, Reznikoff, Darwin, HD, Langston Hughes, Plato, Homer, Dante, Shakespeare and of course, Zukofsky, and so on—a discreet selection of references describing Niedecker's coordinates, her *locus*, her lost & found.

Without preliminaries, the meticulous unobserved observer enters *in medias res* (like New York photographer Helen Levitt, whose special camera fitted with a right-angle viewfinder permitted her to work unnoticed by those who show up in her work[7]), continues her speculations, her "reflections," as she called them, beyond subjectivity. She speaks of the flood from its midst, for like Cezanne, she has the capacity for repeated defamiliarization of "what is there," and is endlessly occupied by it. Mind, bird, war, sky, street, "...a river, impersonally flowing...."[8]

Topologies, dichotomies: "I wonder what the mind will be capable of doing someday without danger to the body?"[9] The structure of particularity whose sound mind names and verbs, notates intervals with tender color, sensuous[10], passionate intellection in a repertoire of motion, its timing and tension fully motivated, activating space.

Extending by re-membering, meaning surprises event. A life/work is shaped by the equation place = "there is nothing else." The choice to live in one's spot, to restrict one's engagement with the social, is the choice to coexist atemporally with a selected cohort of makers and thinkers. This coexistence extends to Niedecker's recuperative use of found materials imbricated with studied dexterity in the immediate, the vernacular of her present, a complex overlapping creating disjunctive order.

Niedecker's choices are not separate from the form they take. "...*poetry has to do it*."[11] Inexorability of the assumptive prerogatives of a dialogic

---

[7] Sandra S. Phillips, "Helen Levitt's New York," in SFMOMA Catalogue *HELEN LEVITT* (SF, 1991) 16.

[8] Jesse Redmon Fauset, *Plum Bun,* excerpted in *The Gender of Modernism,* ed. Bonnie Kime Scott (Indiana, 1990) 167.

[9] Jenny Penberthy, *Niedecker and the Correspondence with Zukofsky 1931-1970* (Cambridge, 1993) 198.

[10] Ibid, 217.

[11] Faranda, 48·

inner speech shapes her acute attention to formal re(ve)lations, causality, chance, change, a strict complexity. The pivotal nature of apostrophe runs through it. Here is someone remembering someone's remembering in the present. "The *tone* of the thing. And awareness of everything influencing everything."[12]

Language is the body's last symptom. "...a rhythm of emergence and secrecy sets in, a kind of watermark of the imaginary."[13] The poet sits in the "anxious seat."[14] The hand gives up the writing. The person in the poem is someone else. Naming echos. The nothing, like the magician's hand, conducts the something lost in the flood. Puzzle rejects closure: prosody tells this story. Although words may refer, the poem, like the subject, has no referent, for it does not pre-exist itself. Rather, it predicts itself, calls itself into being by means of calling or being. Indivisible, it cannot be regional.

Lorine Niedecker was born 12 May 1903, Fort Atkinson, Wisconsin. Except for a few brief excursions (to New York, and on driving trips to further her knowledge of Wisconsin and neighboring states) she lived mostly on Blackhawk Island, Jefferson County, Wisconsin. She died 31 December 1970 in a hospital in Madison, Wisconsin.

now live in music
now read in peace, Lorine[15]

CONJUNCTIONS: 29
Tributes
(Fall 1997)

---

[12] Lorine Niedecker, letter to Gail Roub, 1967, in "Getting to Know Lorine Niedecker," Gail Roub, in *Lorine Niedecker: Woman and Poet,* edited by Jenny Penberthy (Orono, 1996)

[13] Jeane Baudrillard, "The Ecstasy of Communication," in Baudrillard, *The Ecstasy of Communication* (NY, 1988) 33.

[14] John Brinkerhoff Jackson, "The Sacred Grove in America," in Jackson, *The Necessity for Ruins* (Amherst, 1980) 85

[15] Norma Cole, *MARS* (Berkeley, 1994) 19.

Giving up the Private Property of the Self, or the Alienation Effect in Poets' Theater

"But I don't need the money a can opener franchise might net me. This face (touches her face), rumor'd to have been Sodom, has been my meal ticket for many moons. But now Fellini is here, in this house. I feel my doom drawing round me, close, like a particular, vacant picture by Robert Ryman, like these walls all white and pink, like puff pastry. Can you help me, Steve?"

This is Barbara Steele, from Kevin Killian's play, "Three on a Match," from my script, with a hand-drawn slash and comma between "particular" and "vacant," the words "like these walls" written in by the author, a last-minute revision.

"Alienating an event or character," wrote Bertolt Brecht, "means first of all stripping the event of its self-evident, familiar, obvious quality and creating a sense of astonishment and curiosity about them."

In Poets' Theater as I have experienced it, the contradictory nature of cultural, social and political contexts, as well as subjectivity itself, is foregrounded. Ideas of causality, unity, sequence and categorization are turned inside out and stand revealed. Rules of convention and correctness are material to be interrogated, as are theatrical norms and other expectations.

In scratch productions with few rehearsals, the making, construction, scaffolding, the raw materials of the theatrical event are asserted—by all the participants—the edges, margins neither frayed nor boundless but rather unbound. In this universe resolution does not reduce to totalization.

In the first place, the daily working lives of the participants in the production are asserted in the primary evidence: The Script. The Script is present, on the stage, in the hand, a ubiquitous character, a common denominator saying first of all, "This is writing, this is written." There are of course exceptions, where actors learn lines, but for the most part, the script is onstage playing a dual role.

Poets' Theater makes a commitment to the creative nature of lived experience in context. The context is not illusion. Not only that, as the individual skills and talents of participants become known, they are acknowledged and incorporated into productions—the productions expand to build themselves around these abilities. Potentialities are welcomed and thrive. Thus the work of Poets' Theater is the least alienated labor imaginable.

This brings us to the aspect of ensemble work.

"One might say that everything hangs on the 'story' which is what happens *between* people." (Brecht)

The projects of Poets' Theater are communal. They accrete and gather momentum, a kind of critical mass, building on local relationships in time. Someone is writing—often the "someone" is a composite, a dyad, the multiple author—writing for known members of the future cast so the future is here and now. So even the primary or originary moment of writing is expansive, interactive, a function of the vitality of ongoing conversations in a community. The boundaries of the community are permeable and shifting, since it consists of singularities, to use Agamben's term. Individuals express interest in participating. This interest is incorporated. So the dynamics of the participants, a kind of multiple person, or mega-organism live in solution in continuous flux.

And the story inheres in the relationships. The individual participants "learn" each other and play to and with each other. This unfolding in any given play and over time through the sequences of plays becomes an objective exposition of social process, candid and revelatory.

This acting out of roles, our roles, drawing on everyday behavior, sequences, tableaux of everyday life recontextualized, presents a kind of social and cultural citation which is exposition. We quote our actions—and the actions of others—from memory rather than from empathy: "I am going through the motions of characters." We try each other, play each other, the ensemble or cast going through the social motions, excerpting and recombining, thus exposing and questioning. It is collective art practice as well as an extension of the social.

Bodily presence, body language, including the script, holding and maneuvering with a script, moving while reading, not so simple, provides an unusual situation for the language of gesture, unrehearsed in these new combinations, naïve and awkward, willing vulnerability, a relief from the confines of default sophistication, a refreshing and stimulating defamiliarization.

We are onstage, and we are in the audience. In this playful juggling of theatrical conventions, the conventional separation of audience from stage is erased—or rather, from the outset, problematized, put into quotation marks, made more palpable through the suggestion of the possibility of erasure which is really the opposite of erasure or a now-you-see-it-now-you-don't function of performance.

One extension of this permeability inheres in how functions can change, reverse, merge at any time. That is, actor is writer, writer is director—any combination can ensue. The flexibility of situation accommodates all possible contributing impulses. The willingness of the multiple entity, the ensemble, supports all of the above.

The Poets' Theater Jubilee is an extraordinary example of this support. Poets who have not written plays are writing, have written them, people who have not previously directed plays are directing them. Some of the actors are the usual suspects, and some are newcomers to the experience. This would be the moment for us to acknowledge the impresarios of the festival, Kevin Killian and Camille Roy. And it would be the moment to acknowledge the individuals and organizations who run the arts spaces where the rehearsals and the performances take place. And of course this is a celebration for and by all the participants, including audiences, who make the Poets' Theater exist.

To return to the initial quote from "Three on a Match"—

That night we performed the play twice, back to back, to full houses crowded onto chairs and benches in Rick Jacobsen's KIKI gallery on 14th St. Between the performances, players and audience mingled on the sidewalk, joking and flirting, enjoying the evening. Rick Jacobsen has since died of AIDS, his gallery is gone, but we remember him and his endeavors. For some of us he will always be associated with his support of Poets' Theater. This is one instance of the countless cooperative collaborative interarts events Poets' Theater has been part of.

The group work of Poets' Theater resonates for me in particular with the group translation projects I have been involved with. There is the same open opportunity to participate. The limits of the self become permeable, a composite entity, temporary, appears, then disappears, dissolves when the time of the project is at an end. It is an expansive, inclusive embrace. As Zukofksy said of poetry, it is "for the interested."

From personal experience, I can attest to the fact that the undertaking, once begun, becomes an adventure, a life-enhancing …addiction! Once upon a time, many years ago, Kevin Killian surprised me by inviting me to take a tiny role in a play (—name?—) in which I would be Alberta, Elvis's maid. What is it to perform someone else's written words? As if the words are never not someone else's? I read the script over and over, defamiliarization! I practiced my lines, came to rehearsal, and then—the shock of addressing the other—relating!—there was a dynamic between the character I was playing, and the other, or others in the scene. There was tension. Dynamic tension! There were RELATIONSHIPS! The unpredictable ineffable had entered in a big way. It was revelatory. Since then I have never turned down the opportunity to take part.

And this is my personal moment to publicly thank Kevin for his special contribution, his ongoing devotion to Poets' Theater.

Thank you.

(The source for the Brecht material is Peter Brooker's "Key Words in Brecht's Theory and Practice," a chapter in the *Cambridge Companion to Brecht*.)

Poets' Theater Panel
New Langton Arts
San Francisco, Feb. 2, 2002

Goldie & Ruby: A Piece of Short Sets

Introduction
When I was invited to participate on this panel
considering the Objectivists in context, it
interested me, as a poet, to inquire into the
nature of other poets' engagement with context.
I was thinking of context as events, conditions,
Zeitgeist, poetics, the world in which one lives
and works, writes.

The two poets whose work I wanted to think about in this way are HD
and George Oppen, not always considered together. But I saw their
contexts merge in the time of the second World War and this interested
me.

Eventually I settled on two poems written exactly twenty years apart,
with others entering, at moments, where they will.

1943–1963

And now we live in the *aftermath** of 11 September 2001. Our frame
has changed. The attention I felt for these works and issues under
consideration became and continues to become all the more acute,
urgent.

---

* *aftermath* (also aftermowth) Second or later mowing; the crop of grass which
springs up after the mowing in early summer.
(see also Aftergrass, Aftercrop)
1834 Southey: "No aftermath has the fragrance and the sweetness of the first crop."
OED.

Goldie and Ruby: A Piece of Short Sets

The tradition of all dead generations weighs like a nightmare on the brain.
                                   Karl Marx, *18ᵗʰ Brumaire*

THE MOTH

I'm a tiny tiny thing
Ever flying in the spring
Round and round a ringaring.
Long ago I was a king,
Now I do this kind of thing
On the wing, on the wing!
Bing!
James Joyce, *Ulysses*, 486

A poem is a made place, a deedless deed that stakes out or constellates
ambiguity without laying claim to it, without attempting to master
or contain it. The singular can be plural. The names we are looking
at, Goldie and Ruby, are singular, specific. They are not address,
not apostrophe but rather place-holder for the missing, embedded
dedication to the disappeared. Not witness but the event itself. In this
action they become plural, frontiers of the written, evidence of the
social and of history, a new story in real time every time the frame or
rhythm of events changes. They are also markers of what cannot be
kept, remembered, even. Oblivion and loss.
We are talking about a poetics of dispossession here.

Writing is a way of reducing the domain of death,
and of answering the anguish the thought of death
causes.
731, Hélène Cixous, *The Exile of James Joyce*. Trans. Sally A.J. Purcell.
NY: David Lewis 1972

Contextual shaping is *grammar* according to Gregory Bateson. It's an
interesting way to approach "context" in relation to writing poetry in
that contextual shaping seems to indicate an external force or action
or influence whereas grammar is internal, infrastructure, structure. So
the external and the internal are not only congruent but also are not

separate, separable. They are only separable as they need to be in talking about them.

Today I'm going to consider this contextual-shaping-as-grammar in relation to HD and George Oppen, in particular as it can be examined in two poems written about twenty years apart, during circumstances of extreme crisis and upheaval. External event enjoins a poetics, a particular grammar. Here it is the grammar of a kind of divestment, elsewhere called "poverty," "sincerity" or "sympathy." En route, this grammar creates myth, we/readers see myth forming—not narrative, but rather in the erasure of narrative, the movement of thought, the forming of mythic loci of light and shade, destruction, battle, vandals at the gates, hero/heroine/anti-hero parthenogenesis, exchange of "I" and "you" positions, regeneration, elegy and praise.

Contextual shaping, the context is grammar, grammar is ground, grounding. What almost broke George and Mary up was Mary's lack of grammar, suddenly apparent when she began to write "her book," her "our life." Oppen's book of *Collected Poems* bears the dedication "for Mary// whose words in this book are entangled/ inextricably among my own." As for her mangled grammar, he advised her to get a grammar book, a context, other than his own.

Like Rauschenberg, Oppen uses newsprint, "the news" as contextual grammar, tracking of shadow and light, psychic priming coalescing with myth, the myth of the frontier, the plains, the hero, the anti-hero—as HD has used the grammar of experience. Her trial-by-fire experience-text includes love, wars, books, cinema, travel—both making their work through a process of erasure and condensation, the form holding, strengthening as the context thickens into tensile frame.

A musical element, a little song or magic chant, celebration or elegy, interrupts the tracking of thought, the solemnity of thought unfolding in all inconclusiveness.

I am speaking of the procedure of montage: the superimposed element disrupts the context in which it is inserted....Only interruption here has not the character of a stimulant but an organizing function.

Walter Benjamin, "The Author as Producer"

You may say this is no poem
but I
will remember this hour
till I die.
HD 492

Weaving the short lines together, I is I till I die. Time is the medium, ground, foreground, agent. Time is plural, finite and infinite. Time and the poem stand in for one another. Something is something else. I can be you or she. This has often been true in HD's syntax of equation. Not metaphor, it's real, she's 56. I is a time-coordinate in the matrix of the poem. So is

the wall-door under the chestnut tree
that I nor anyone else ever saw open,
opens and lets out a carpenter:
...
he mends the broken window-frame of the orangery,
I mend a break in time.
HD 493

They have tools, they do their work, there is the pleasure of participating in simple joinery, a mending—temporal, temporary?—with a piece of narrative, the *sound* of story.

And futher on,

who was I?
HD 496

which also asks who was that carpenter whose presence defines me, this time?

It is our positioning within space, both as the
point of perspectival access to space, but also
as an object for others in space, that gives the
subject any coherent identity.
Elizabeth Grosz (in V. Burgin, *Some Cities*)

One cannot help but think, here, of Akhmatova's "Requiem," with its prefatory note written April 1, 1957 "in line" as it were, in the trance-line outside a Leningrad prison, the building personalized for her at that time because her son was a prisoner within its walls. A "woman with blue lips" asks, "Can you describe this?" Akhmatova says yes and the woman exhibits the "shadow of a smile."

`Contradictions without concilation; it is not a`
`question of dialectics.`
Blanchot, "Enigma"

this is not a poem
only a day to remember
I say the war is over...
the war is over...
HD 492

The frame exhibits a strength that does not preclude permeability, a kind of porosity, the reader's ticket to "internal cinema."

`...our thoughts clash and sometimes` **`smash`** `our shells...`
HD to May Sarton

This smashing or cracking open that is the work of imagination of a collective called "writer" bears on the collective called "reader."

And it is the breakdowns, the hinges that articulate microworlds, that are
the source of the autonomous and creative side of living cognition.
Francisco Varela, *Ethical Know-How*, 11

In the opening is ... "thought being made in the ear," (Denise Riley) violence, dismemberment, basic elements in pieces implying—repetition and the resistant tension of new form—innovation.

I don't mean he despairs, I mean if he does not
He sees in the way of poetry
George Oppen, *CP* 191,"Route"

Naming, slithering, remembering:

HD writes to Norman Holmes Pearson in 1937 ('A Note on Poetry'):

Poetry? You ask. I am to say, why I wrote, when
I wrote and how I wrote these fragments. I am
to state this simply, for people who may not
altogether be in sympathy with my own sort of
work. I wish I could do that. I am so afraid I
cannot. But the inner world of imagination, the
ivory tower, where poets presumably do live, in
memory, does stand stark with the sun-lit isles
around it, while battle and din of battle and the
whole dreary, tragic spectacle of our times, seems
blurred and sodden, and not to be recalled, save in
moments of reputation, historical necessity. I had
not the power to repudiate at that time or explain.
(Repudiate? Explain?)
But I do so well remember one shock, a letter
from Miss Monroe (Harriet Monroe, founder and first editor of
Poetry: A Magazine of Verse) timed, nicely, to arrive to
greet me, when I had staggered home, exhausted and
half-asphyxiated. (I and my companion had been
shoved off the pavements, protesting to a special
policeman that we would rather be killed on the
pavement than suffocate in the underground.)
Miss Monroe was one of the first to print and
recognize my talent. But how strangely, farcically
blind to our predicament! The letter suggested with
really staggeringly inept solicitude that HD would
do so well, maybe, finally, if she could get into
"life," into the rhythm of our time, in touch with
events and so on and so on and so on. I don't know
what else she said. I was laughing too much.
          Ivory tower?

          That was and is still, I believe with many,
the final indictment of this sort of poetry.

We don't live. We don't see life. And so on.

Oppen will come at this dilemma from the other side of the looking glass in 1964 when he lays out his reasons for writing, for not becoming reinvolved in active political struggle as he had done previously when he left off writing poetry altogether for over two decades, about which he has said, "In a way I gave up poetry because of the pressure of what for the moment I'll call conscience."
George Oppen, Dembo interview

In order to speak adequately of my poetry and its aims, I must, you see, drag in a whole deracinated epoch. Perhaps specifically, I might say that the house next door was struck another night. We came home and simply waded through glass, while wind from now-unshuttered windows, made the house a barn, an unprotected dug-out. What does that sort of shock do to the mind, the imagination— not solely of myself but of an epoch?
HD, 1937

Any *I* seems to speak for and from herself; her utterance comes from her own mouth in the first person pronoun which is hers, if only for just so long as she pronounces it. Yet as a human speaker, she knows that it's also everyone's, and that this grammatical offer of uniqueness is untrue, always snatched away. The *I* which speaks out from only one place is simultaneously everyone's everywhere; it's the linguistic marker of rarity but is always also aggressively democratic.
Denise Riley, *The Words of Selves,* 57

Goldie was one of us
we are one with Goldie
HD 498

Organon, from the Greek (ὀργανο(ν)) instrument, bodily organ, becomes a system of rules or principles of demonstration or investigation, an instrument of thought or knowledge *(OED),* that is to say, how the poet proceeds and what they say about how they proceed.

Vocative, appellative, anapostrophic.

One imagines himself/addressing his peers/I suppose.
George Oppen, *This in Which* 84

no/ no/ no/ what am I saying?
HD 496

To make it look so simple....Rhythms established with chants....Well there
are songs under the gorse
Barbara Guest, "Biography"

The line is eternally under attack. Tension activates the ground.

You cannot paint it today as you painted yesterday.
HD *Paint it Today*

    If one is to move   to experience   further
one needs a syntax, a new syntax   A new syntax
is a new cadence of disclosure, a new cadence of
logic, a new musical cadence
    A new 'structure of space'
(1963 or 1964) George Oppen to Andy Meyer, 97

with all attention to the truth of the moment
Robert Duncan, "Dante Etudes"

Goldie made the words come true
HD 408

Goldie had her picture
in a little exhibition,
Goldie was in the news
for half a second,
Goldie had her little job,
ambulance?
        mobile canteen?
            extra fire-girl?
I don't know,
I only just remember

the caption,
a line and a half,
below the newspaper photograph,
which said:
known as Goldie
because of her
fair
hair,
she was found sitting upright
at the wheel of her emergency car,
dead.
HD 497-8

Imagination is rational thought brought back to the body.
Brian Massumi, *A User's Guide to Capitalism and Schizophrenia*

Little breaths in unexpected places, shock waves. Haptic knowledge, cities, islands, ruins and a shrine open to the air—the erotics of shrine, of ruin. In the ecstasy of ruins apocalypse is always now.

I call it Hellas. I might, psychologically just as well, have listed the Casco Bay Islands off the coast of Maine but I call my islands Rhodes, Samos and Cos.
HD, Letter to Norman Holmes Pearson

Or Dodona, one of the oldest shrines in Greece:

Here am I, your daughter,
Zeus, provider,
I bring millet in a basket,
White-grain
HD 408

Produce, provisions, their urgency, their lack directing daily action during the deprivation of wartime. HD's friend Sylvia Dobson grew produce south of London, in the flight path of the bombers, brought it to the city-ruins-shrine during the war.

Physical psychological symbolic sites: London, Paris, New York, San Francisco, Corfu or Little Deer Island, the Eros/Anteros of place is active. Place—encoded memory and possibility—at times beautiful, mysterious, wanton and unforgiving. Its magnetism structures and suffuses the poem, inflecting scale, measure, atmosphere and line.

Paris—
this city
which taught my generation

Art
and the great paved places
of the cities.
George Oppen, *This in Which,* "Eros" 44, 45

Thursday 16 March, 1939
I see too that Hitler has marched into Prague.
This, says the PM "is not in the spirit of
the Munich agreement." My comment anyhow is
superfluous.
Virginia Woolf, *Diary Vol.5 1936-41* 208

Friday 16 August, 1940
They came very close. We lay down under the tree.
The sound was like someone sawing in the air just
above us. We lay flat on our faces, hands behind
head. Don't close yr teeth said L.
Ibid. 311

The furthest I remember back is being woken by my
mother in the middle of the night. We sat at the
bottom of the stairs, in the narrow hall between
the kitchen and the downstairs room. The front
door was opposite us. A pane of glass set high in
the door showed a rectangle of pale night sky.
As I watched this floating blank page it abruptly
displayed a black cross, trailing fire. Then
nothing. I asked what it was we had seen. 'Father
Christmas in his aeroplane', she said, 'bringing
the toys'. Many years later, I asked again. 'A
doodle-bug', she said, 'a V-1 flying bomb'.
Victor Burgin, *Some Cities.* UC Press 1996

But the five-year 'reality' of bombs, fly-bombs and
V2 was by far the less stable or 'real' than the
world of the imagination….
HD to Aldington, 6 June 1950?

Nothing and no one stops HD from staying with Bryher in their
London apartment with its black-out curtains closed against the war-
night-sky, described thus in fragments from a report by American
journalist Edward R. Murrow, "over in London covering the war":

September 10, 1940
This is London. And the raid which started about
seven hours ago is still in progress. Larry LeSueur
and I have spent the last three hours driving
about the streets of London and visiting air-raid
shelters. We have found that like everything else
in this world, the kind of protection you get from
the bombs on London tonight depends on how much
money you have.

By "protection," he explains, he is referring to physical comfort, not
safety. No one was safe from the bombs, the fires, whether it be those
in a Mayfair hotel lobby or under canvas in a trench cut into public
parkland.

Murrow continues,
Once I saw "The Damnation of Faust" presented in
the open air at Salzburg. London reminds me of that
tonight, only the stage is so much larger.

And the next day,
Military medals are getting rather meaningless
in this war. So many acts of heroism are being
performed by men (sic) who were just doing their
daily job. And now, at 4:20 in the morning we're
just waiting for the all-clear.

Men like the young woman hero Goldie, who

… wouldn't move away.
Goldie was told to stay.
HD 497, 499

a repeated refrain shifting conditions.

In "May 1943," in a poem that is a "mending" in time, "mending time,"
HD writes

this is not a poem
only a day to remember,
I say the war is over...
the war is over...

What is this as an act? As an everyday (might one say) *mantra*? Stage
direction? Memory of the happy ghost of the previous war's ending?
Is it here that HD marks the poet's becoming her own muse? Own
muse=own scribe?

A seed is not a crystal—and if my mustard seed has
grown too high and spread too many branches, that
is a pity for the critic...Now here it is at the
last—a sort of vindication of the writer or the
"scribe."
HD to Norman Holmes Pearson (in *Trilogy*, vi)

the bone frame was made for
no such shock knit within terror,
yet the skeleton stood up to it:

the flesh? It was melted away.
The heart burnt out, dead ember,
tendons, muscles, shattered, outer husk dismembered,

yet the frame held:
we passed the flame: we wonder
what saved us? What for?
HD *Trilogy* 4

"Is the frame holding," asks Lily ("The Grifters").

The frame holds, opens new space, commemorating event.

August 9, 1964
Your phrase, the creative now—is a name of what
I've known for a long time now that I must manage.
The phrase becomes one of the seed phrases. First
one—what—one 'grows roots' as they say, but we
really want to say 'shares roots'
          and meanwhile, the 'creative now'—the tip
leaf which is oneself growing into a 'new space.'
Frightening and not frightening, not as frightening
as if one weren't.
George Oppen to June

Oppen has said, in his interview with Dembo that in a way he gave
up poetry because of the pressure of what for the moment he called
conscience. And now, in the letters we see him examine his division
of time, his decision to write no matter what. Again, a decision of
conscious conscience.

          I think I divide my time differently from
most people. And perhaps not particularly wisely.
I did only the one thing for twenty years. And now
I want desperately to get my own work done. I talk
about other things, and I think about other things,
including Goldwater. But the fact is that if the
White Citizens council or chinese invaders burned
this house down, I would pick up my typewriter and
my note book and move elsewhere if I could.
Ibid.

On August 8, 1964 he writes to his daughter Linda,

I just try to hang on to the principle that I have
only one life and I've done a number of things and
right now I want very much to do this, to write
poetry. God knows if one has a 'right,' but I think
it is what I am going to do. I really will not be
able to face the idea of not having done it.

But trouble came.
Book of Job 3.28

Why *now*, why is George Oppen coming up against this decision, already taken, and agonizing over it again, now?

"You know," says (Richard "Mickey") Flacks, "the summer of '63 was a very, very optimistic moment, probably the peak moment for my generation. The nuclear-test-ban treaty was about to be signed. The civil rights movement was at a peak of exuberant pressure and protest. And Kennedy had made his speech at American University." The liberal agenda seemed open to change. Ordinary people were in political motion for the first time since the Thirties. Even the popular culture seemed full of portent. As Flacks and Hayden rejoiced, Bob Dylan's 'Blowin' in the Wind' had become a Top Ten hit. James Miller, *Democracy is in the Streets: From Port Huron to the Siege of Chicago.* 182–3, 395n52

Of course it wasn't Bob's version but a more commercially acceptable i.e. anodyne version by Peter, Paul and Mary.

One lived an extreme of something. From within that geodesic dome of the present, one could not foresee exactly what was to come. But the unusual degree of activity would resonate powerfully with Oppen's progressive/subversive/activist life experience.

August 28, 1963, March on Washington for Jobs and Freedom, the largest political demonstration in U.S. history to that date. James Baldwin reports:

That day, for a moment, it almost seemed that we stood on a height, and could see our inheritance; perhaps we could make the kingdom real, perhaps the beloved community would not forever remain the dream one dreamed in agony.

Steven Kasher, *The Civil Rights Movement: A Photographic History* 122

But agony was the common denominator in this grammar of events. Sunday September 15, 1963, Youth Day, the bombing of the Sixteenth Street Baptist Church in Birmingham. Denise McNair, Carole Robertson, Cynthia Wesley and Addie Mae Collins were blown to their deaths. (See Spike Lee's documentary "4 Little Girls") On a New York television program James Baldwin says, "Most Americans don't have any longer a real sense of what they live by. I really think it may be Coca Cola."

Shall we relinquish

Sanity to redeem
Fragments and fragmentary
Histories in the towns and the temperate streets
Too shallow still to drown in or mourn
The courageous and precarious children
George Oppen, "The Impossible Poem," *CP* 226

And then the disappearance of Mickey Schwerner, James Chaney
and Andrew Goodman, civil rights workers who were murdered in
Mississippi while setting up a freedom school and participating in the
voter registration drive. Days after their disappearance, on the CBS
Evening News Walter Cronkite called the search for the three—found
nine months later, buried in a Klansman's dam—"the focus of the whole
country's concern."

Disorder and disruption.
Oppen names names, proposes relationships, the new syntax in
which meaning accrues. Job and Mickey Schwerner, Mets fan. One
imagines Oppen would have known Nathan Schwerner, Mickey's
father, another "subversive" from New York. The *Selected Letters* include
correspondence between Oppen and Armand Schwerner, poet and also
a cousin of the murdered young man. This particular loss is close to
home. Context shapes the grammar of lament-as-*éloge*, praise and elegy
in the one French word.

éloge, from

        eulogos, both "eloquent" and "reasonable"
and from

        eulogia, blessing
after

        eu legein, to speak well of

what image would I choose
had I one thing, as gift,
redeemed from dust and ash?
HD "Christmas 1944"

Local terror, new site where news recombines with other matter, forming distillate, new matter. Oppen's poem, "THE BOOK OF JOB AND A DRAFT OF A POEM TO PRAISE THE PATHS OF THE LIVING" begins

image   the images

The newspaper and TV images of the moment, in black and white and living color, broadcast worldwide, were of beatings of civil rights workers by police, by the Klan, often one and the same, water cannons, dogs, bomb-sites and bodies. Terror makes history and the memory of the unwritten.
These lines, all lowercase, these spaces a sign of respect to the dead? With whip-like enjambment—of conscience?—the poet demands

...what is the form
to say it there is something
to name   Goodman   Schwerner   Chaney
who were beaten not we
who were beaten   children
not our
children   ancestral
children rose in the dark
to their work...

The Book of Job, 5.4 (King James Version) tells us *"His children are far from safety, and they are crushed in the gate, neither is there any to deliver them."*

And the silences structure the lament. Despair comes into the spaces. Not that the poet despairs, that is something else. Otherness, becoming other, "dispersion" (HD's word), dispossession, danger.

...because history is nothing but the différance of revolution....
Giorgio Agamben, *Idea of Prose* 23

For HD and Oppen their art is act in time, incorporating extremes of song and open form, social, public. In accordance with Raymond Williams's equation between ideology and "the conditions of all conscious life," each work occurs from the abstract of personal experience into a concretion, in this instance the written. Thus one might imagine that the poem "is where the deep structures of society actually reproduce themselves as conscious life." Raymond Williams, "Crisis in English Studies."

Or as Don DeLillo's character David Ferrie puts it, "Whatever you set your mind to, your personal total obsession, this is what kills you. Poetry kills you if you're a poet." This from his novel, *Libra*, which focuses on events around the Kennedy assassination of 22 November, 1963, and especially on Oswald, the alleged assassin who was shot— live, on TV—by Jack Ruby.

Oppen's immediate response is preserved in a letter to June Oppen Degnan dated Nov. 24, 1963 where it is evident that he does not believe Oswald was the shooter and he does imagine a conspiracy involving the Dallas Police.

        There is at least in 'everyone's' mind—I
suppose I mean the intellectuals—that something
very violent is going on, and that perhaps they
are fools. We begin to remember again how much we
really do care, how much we have at stake, how very
endangered we are, how far we are from the belt-
buckled semi-fascist population, and how close we
are to each other. The a-principled Kennedy, the
half-educated liberal-arts major, the academic Alan
Dugan, the weak liberal, the disturbed radical—
Perhaps something like this might be felt. That it
is—simply—again a period of crisis.
George Oppen, *SL* 95-6

As soon as the Warren Commission Report is available, Oppen reads it and writes to Linda and Alex Mourelatos, on September 30, 1964, that he is completely convinced that it has been thorough and that there was no conspiracy. He is convinced by the prosody.

And I thought this report far beyond anything I
know in literature—surely beyond anything I know of
in prose: overwhelming, haunting, inescapable.
George Oppen, *SL* 95-6

```
Chapter VI is perhaps the most startling, because
we do have a precedent for it in Bloomsday. It
follows with startling closeness, which is a
tribute to Joyce, but this is far beyond anything
in Ulysses.
```
George Oppen, *SL* 95-6

Oppen continues in great detail describing Ruby-Blooms' movements.

```
The river flows through Bloom's day. But everything
comes together on Ruby's head in that newspaper
office….Like Bloom talking to Stephen, Ruby cannot
understand his final act. Because, as he said,
a Zero, a Nothing had caused this event, someone
must act, he thought. And from somewhere in his
background he thought that a Jew, a Jewish man, a
'man of the Jewish faith—and it is so stupid…and I
never use the term'—must act.
```

In a postscript to this letter Oppen states that the parallel is "more than a literary curiosity for us: *Ulysses* is so deep in our lives. It was the first modern literature we read, it was our education." And he establishes kinship. "And it was the beginning of our lives together//—I guess it was Lindy's grandfather."

From the *Warren Commission Report*, which, in Chapter VI, describes "Ruby's Activities From November 21 to November 24, 1963" in great detail.

```
Detective Augustus M. Eberhardt, who also recalled
that he first saw Ruby earlier in the evening,
said Ruby carried a notepad and professed to be
a translator for the Israeli Press. He remembered
Ruby's remark how unfortunate the assassination
was for the city of Dallas and that it was "hard to
realize that a complete nothing, a zero like that,
could kill a man like President Kennedy…."
```
Warren Commission Report

to the poem, "Armies of the Plain."

Twenty-four years after Oppen's poem, DeLillo writes,
There is also the Warren Report, of course, with its twenty-six accompanying
volumes of testimony and exhibits, its millions of words. Branch thinks this
is the megaton novel James Joyce would have written if he'd moved to Iowa
city and lived to be a hundred....

Everything is here.... This is the Joycean book of America, remember—the
novel in which nothing is left out.
DeLillo, *Libra* 181-2

Forty years earlier, Joyce had written *Ulysses* where, aside from the
association, the conflation of the two men, the two "characters," Bloom
and Ruby, you may recall that the Nighttown episode *is*, as it were, shot
through with rubies:

(Tenderly, as he slips on her finger a ruby ring.)
James Joyce, *Ulysses* 423
I now introduce Mademoiselle Ruby, the pride of the ring.
Ibid. 431
(Bloom assumes a mantle of cloth of gold and puts on a ruby ring.)

There is a diversion here. Another instance of mythmaking before the
Myth of the Blaze invents itself.

From the letter of November 24, 1963:
     Seeing the photos of Jacqueline Kennedy with
her children—the silly Vassar make-up removed—one
realizes what a very beautiful young woman she
is, and recognizes her strength and honor. And the
children stand quietly, and one remembers that
such children understand speech and honor and it
has been possible to tell them that they must
behave honorably—. And they stand quietly with
their mother. Perhaps we will have to understand
all this, and that perhaps all such people are
endangered in the present world.

Oppen's works build their lexicon, simultaneously building myth. Known for his love of the little words, one forgets at times to attend to his other words such as *frontier* and *plains*. As well as bearing the history of colonization, occupation and genocide in North America, the pioneer whole cowboy past, *frontier* at that time would also refer to the cold war "new frontier," space, the "space race," competition with Sputnik to be the first to plant a flag on the moon, claim the moon. As for the *plains*, their presence under the asphalt, under cities such as Chicago, is thoroughly discussed in the Dembo interview. The description of the widow and her family occurs at the moment when Jacqueline Kennedy relays to Theodore White the Kennedy-Camelot bedtime story. Oppen is present, as midwife in a way, at the birth of the myth that will characterize a thousand days.

that's Swan of Avon logic
writes HD ("May 1943")

which is to say, not direct treatment of the thing but rather experience inflected and given *sense* by context, by syntax, completely located in this story of history far from the image of "Imagism," the object of "Objectivism." The reader is interpolated into the "us" of history, the assumptions of shared experience beyond phenomenology, beyond fact.

Underneath all, individuals,
I swear nothing is good to me now that ignores individuals
    Whitman, *Leaves of Grass (1891-92)*

Talk delivered at the Modernist Studies Association,
Rice University, October 15, 2001

"of theory / of possibility"

A— *"I did sweet fuck all about it."*
B—*"It's so forced."*
A—"Is that bad?"

The state had come to us fragmentary. Our writing was unavoidable.

Some readers have trouble distinguishing between theory as θεωρηα, something to be looked at, spectacle, speculation, "theory," propositions to be proved,
and
theory as predigested, predictable form, restricted forms. Now Derridean knock-offs are all the rage. "The hunger for catechism," it was called by Alexander Wat in *My Century.*

This is the broadcast zone. "The earth remained fixed and without motion." (Cicero, *The Good Life*) "…except that Silence works alone…." (Heldris de Cornuälle / Lewis Thorpe, *Le Roman de Silence*)

Here are the complete sentences. Eat what you open. Heat it up. Raise your voice when you sleep on it.

How will she edit herself?

How will she censor herself?

Such were the terms of the peace that in name we share a language, "theory its own jocular reader." (*Mace Hill Remap*) Come to it individually and into community. Reading each other we authorize each other.

call	The situation in the arena of theory
it	is congruent with situations
influence,	of social, economic, political
visibility, etc.	cultural, etc., arenas.

"brother and sister in at least one / other language is said in one word"
(My Bird Book). What are the limits of this naming, this saying?

She just wanted to get back to the city. She wouldn't stand for anything
else. Since our full mobility devolves from our concerns, necessity is not
the same as literality.

Willed and willing. History puts words in our mouths. We make
history.

There are different explanations for the laughter, for the huge meals.
Ultimately you are at home with your decision.

Women / Writing / Theory
Raddle Moon (#11, 1992)

Untitled (M)

How soon this will happen
is another question. *

100% on the floor, pieces of paper or scraps of light. Birds, as though
wanting it louder. Cartwheels, three volumes, so probably earlier. It
shapes everything. There is in their existence a letter. A thing needing
no explanation. 100% can't find the letter now, so must have dreamed
it. At first there was a physical approval. Circumstances, the materials at
hand. How often does any negotiation
                         Who could say—
"I have for the moment everything I need"?
          all the time and in the while

Experience does not care, for it comprises a unified theory of the senses.

To verify the symptom of limbs.

The territory and all its subterranean properties
               underneath "Cartesia" the territory
     in its entirety
all the while the territory
and its introduction. Its interruption

                         Having forgotten it too well *

thoughts, feelings and
decisions were accompanied
by fleas, lice and since
it was impossible to
get rid of them
except by burning
the cities, though often
that was done for
other reasons

("Momma what's this?" The little boy in the dream asking about the
blood—on his finger, he touches my cheek with it. It's from his face, his

nose has been bleeding. There is some blood around his nostrils. He has
come to me, his "strategy" to call me or someone "momma" and see if
she will be that.
notebook, 28.iv.97

"He touches his face then touches your cheek leaving a red mark.
Momma what is that he says. Are their gestures not thoughts?" ("My
Operatives")

> *For both were blinded. Of course,*
> *this is mere fancy; one can see such*
> *distant times only in fancy's light.**

The measure of the field is everything you remember plus everything
they remember. Language and the thoughts of people are inseparable.
Take away where things merge as they do in life and in the mind
substitute logic, the line with above and below. Remote from memory,
the memory closing—how can such a state know memory? Evidence of
the investigation. The future opens tomorrow, they said.

> *...the thought of it becomes*
> *unendurable, except in flashes.**

Stanzas overlooking increased
seeing
              There were children
and then the children
were
              The children
are gods+there is no final
analysis=the double displacement
open-ended to thought+the effect
of the montage=something like if only
they could keep it up+people fear
what requires watching=the illusion
that presence could defer
the inevitable

Here is the falling down, or there? What was the first person? The clock? What it ate? Terror? Across gesture? When reading did you come across "strategies" that you could relate/connect to what we've been given? What if we'd been shaped to the contrary? Or finally worked in relation to the contrary?

Take a point accurate to it. Bring in questions, material. Deductible questions. Paraphasia: "language of the father." Pick her up today. That is why "thought are things—sometimes they are songs." (HD) Wanting exercise. The address of same. Examine the linens to see what we owe. A Shakespeare collar helps.

(The generations were E, and J who was sleeping and not going to awake, there but gone; 100%; and W who fell out of the car when 100% opened the door from the outside, unexpectedly, since he had already gotten out and was going home. But he opened the door and W fell out, fell down on his face. 100% picked him up and quickly handed him to {}—he was alright, just a tiny spot of blood on his cheek, a scrape.
notebook 20.iv.97

"By design he fell out of the truck so I picked him up. There was one little spot of blood on his cheek. Someone had opened the door from without." ("My Operatives")

Out of phase—there (the only place) to go or to be. As the writers of these loves, they are the powers.

*As for the warriors**

Everything comes true. This is only the story and not excluding others. So, you are reading the air. For some, it is like reeling in some film or other. That love and care are insufficiently theorized like the rest of experience. A bird was repeating the bell-like sound. Experience does not care about preparation. And so, although our contradictions differ, they feel, and it is an unusual engagement. The chips are down. We will need this and that. Falling off a log as acute sensation. Local effects among themselves. And to think "see the world with your eyes," a vividness.

Or blankness. Tiny pair of lungs. Attendance is the epitome of something. This is where it begins. "Did you ever drop the baby?" she asks, flinging it about. A gathering of membranous edging on each side. Now the heartbreak of the rational. One can always find another pen or pencil. One story keeps busting in on another.

Site of precipitation. That's not memory it's a picture as though it is still a possible action shaking like the idea of a leaf. The jump between light and the understanding of it. "But the Sybil, I saw her hanging there...." Or water and a few seeds. Can experience be a false bottom? Silence reports event, moment builder. Emergence, the beanstalk, the idea of "finding." And the firelight, flickering. Meaning like action takes soundings on positions. And down we go.

(Dream of T alive as form.)

*The moments of grace are rare**

"I have sixpence in my heart, or at least a sliver of ice," she said. "A corkscrew, screwpull—PULL—an ashtray." Then he counted his money.

Experience contributes to the common fund. Silence unsettles the spoken things. Be good for nothing, be still. And not announce these numbers and not between and nothing here at all.

The Grand Permission: New Writings on Poetics and Motherhood,
eds. Brenda Hillman & Patricia Dienstfrey
(Wesleyan University Press, 2003)

---

*Simone Weil, *The ILIAD or the Poem of Force*. Trans. Mary McCarthy. Wallingford, PA: Pendle Hill, 1956

NINES AND TENS: A TALK ON TRANSLATION

I will tell you a terrible secret: language is punishment.
It must encompass all things and in it all things must again
transpire according to guilt and the degree of guilt.

—Ingeborg Bachmann

The translation never takes place since the texts have nothing in
common. The words are all different.
Leap of faith.
Transcendence or encounter.
A record of the encounter. What is hidden and common to both. Nine
nights. Ten nights.
Nine, *nones*, the prayer offered at the ninth hour, the Latin *nona hora*;
origin of noon. *Nonariae* (in ancient Rome, prostitutes were called
nonariae because their doors opened at nine).
Ten, a tithe, based on the ancient Jewish form adopted by both
Christians and Romans, a tenth part of the harvest, *decimus*, what was
due. Decimate meant exacting punishment from every tenth man in the
legion.
In Bugilai, New Guinea, the "number word" is the word for a specific
body part. The body part becomes conventionalized as the number's
name: nine, *ngama*, left breast. Ten, *dala*, right breast. For Torres Strait
Islanders, nine is sternum, ten left shoulder. In Papua, New Guinea,
nine is right ear, ten right eye. Paraguay: nine, arrived at the other hand,
two sides alike. Ten, finished, the hands. In the Zuni language, nine is
ten-a-li-k'ya, all but one held up with the rest. Ten is *äs-tem-'thla*, all of
the fingers.
The nine is imprisoned in the ten. The ten is implied by the nine.
There is red in the pink and they are distinct.
What, if anything, is the poem assuming? Supposing? Besides the words
themselves, what could there be?
In a received world, the sign itself is nothing. Retrieve a morsel and
build a meal around it. You mean steal, but steal what, Prometheus?
This then is the crime. It has its suspense. To some extent, or in a
certain way, we are all one-trick ponies. We do what we can.

We did what we could.

We did that which we have could. (*Fr.*)

We have what we could done. (*Ger.*)

It casts back difference, the shadow you are walking in. You attempt to draw a dotted line around that shadow, an outline.

An outside.

An aside. There is a local painter who appropriates shapes from popular culture, from, say, magazine ads. The shapes are often of women, "heavily coded." The artist then has friends, other artists, perhaps, assume these positions. The artist will then use these new images, these translations. What could these translations say about the originals? If the viewer a) is, b) is not, fluent in the original language.

"translate to keep the damage."

Present what it is in the way of presenting what it is not.

Make a shape around that by what is. Mirror to it its worst nightmare.

Experience the inevitability of violence, the violence of being excluded or expelled from the space, violence of ice.

An implied quest. There will be a struggle.

What kind of crime could it be? A theft? Of what?

A quest or a theft. There will be a struggle.

Retracing a production, starting with a reading. A going towards, backwards.

If a word can be replaced by any other word, what is the shape or space into which these words configure?

Now that we no longer have the sewing machine on the operating table, now that we no longer have to raise metaphors from birth, we have the wasp, and the orchid, we have Rimbaud and Beckett, "Le Bâteau ivre," and "Drunken Boat,"

the nine and the ten.

There is no original of the encounter, only the encounter representing itself. The nine and the ten are close enough but not the same and can't help each other.

> La tempête a béni mes éveils maritimes.
> Plus léger qu'un bouchon j'ai dansé sur les flots
> Qu'on appelle rouleurs eternels de victimes,
> Dix nuits, sans regretter l'oeil niais des falots.
> > —*from "Le Bâteau ivre" by Arthur Rimbaud*

I started awake to tempestuous hallowings.

Nine nights I danced like a cork on the billows, I danced

On the breakers, sacrificial, for ever and ever,
And the crass eye of the lanterns was expunged.
—*from "Drunken Boat,"*
Beckett's translation of "Le Bâteau ivre"

The first unanswered question, after all, or before all, really, is how
does the listening get translated into seeing, into writing, the material
visibility that exists. This is the first translation, or could be, a model
translation, depending on transcendence. Not that all writing comes
from hearing, or overhearing. There is the writing generating itself from
its own materiality. Space for time.

to transform what began as reading into a crime
—*Benjamin Hollander,*
"In the Extreme of Translation: 'writing without
writing': the character of an encrypted wound"

Is it—language—makeshift after all? But then, makeshift for what?
What makes this circling, this avoiding—this this that is the
'talking around' language is—come through, surround us?—*Ibid.*
Avoid "avoidance," all in parenthesis, and propose instead, in the
territory described by Julia Kristeva, the chora, process far more violent,
more of a struggle, an engagement different from the walking-around
avoidance is. Than the emptying out, the draining. There is a life-and-
death struggle between the fire and the lid.
Perhaps the very attempt to "put the lid on it," to make the choices,
write the writing, all choices, is a way at the same time to make more
visible the empty space, the vacancy. However, we are finding a lot of
action in this vacancy, activity that is not at the point of condensation.
"Boiling point" would imply transcendence. Here we say "condensation"
for the coolness of the surface. It is so cool that we say "we" for "I" here.
"Doesn't the translator—doesn't his (sic) translation not only say 'see,
this is what I heard'…" (Hollander) and then expanding, we translators
add, "see, this is some of what I read…" This is evidence of the struggle,
this is what has surfaced.
Hollander's avoidance, André du Bouchet's "inattention," are descriptions
of reading. Is reading the crime. As Hollander says, reading is creating
a fiction of one's own. As someone said, as one translator writing his
memoirs about translation said, how pleasant to recreate one's own
experience of reading for the poor reader who can't read it in its pristine
original form.

How pleasant to live in a fiction of one's own. Or what a bloody nightmare.
The judges go out onto the ice and examine the traces. The audience, at greater distance, imagines the traces.
"…and, in effect, nothing more was heard." (Mallarmé)
Or meaning as product, product of combining words, making meaning specific, particular, local, what did not preexist the combination. Untranslatable there. What becomes translatable there becomes the idea of meaning. The way a recorded performance of music communicates, for all to hear, for all time (until it is buried in the sand), the idea of the performance, which is, in itself, an idea (translation) of the music *as it is written.*
Everything begins to appear as inscription, caption. What is under or underneath. What is neath.
One of the twins identified what is socially coded as glamour as "fear of." He was a sociopath, a killer whose taxonomy did not need to distinguish between amphibious and reptilian. Was this a kind of personal transcendence. He had to literalize the murder. This was his crime.
Emile Benveniste writes, in *Problems of General Linguistics*, about the power struggle that is central to the study of semiotics itself, herself. At a certain point, interest is pulled to the general, the rule, the language template, obliterating concern for the specific relations of denotation. On top of this will to order, to make transcendent order, semiotics denies that she is doing it. "It," in the French, read "she," renews metaphysics' imperialism, ever drawn towards transcendence. "She/it belongs to the family of grandiose projects."
Materiality and praxis go together.

Israelis Kill 6 Armed Arabs Entering I

By JOEL BRINKLEY
Special to The New York Times

JERUSALEM, March 11 — Israeli troops shot and killed six heavily armed Arab gunmen who had crossed the border from Jordan this morning, hours before Secretary of State James A. Baker 3d arrived for talks in ded to foster Arab-Israeli pe als said.

The army said the largest an tempt ent They

In Israel, blood is spilled mi lk of peace.

ment officials announced that Mr. Baker had canceled his tour of Jerusa-'s Old City, which had been sched- his afternoon, because they here was too

immigr ing Mi charge migrat Mr. S ernmen tive to t'

Durin noon at testers "Bak "You w Soo Ur

hypogram, *New York Times*, 12/3/91

Hypogrammatically is one way to read, not deliberate, beside the point in that it might be inadvertent. Total materiality, visuality of language breaking out of conventions, out of "The Code." The genotext is busting out all over.

Saussure went from studying Saturnian verse metrically, prosodically, to scientifically combing this body of verse for the text within the text, for visual figures embedded within the text, like Jakobson's sound figures. And then, doing what he was so compelled always to do, proposed rules, the set of rules at work here.

Rules, extrapolated ordering principles, aspire to govern. At any rate, we have a set of them because Saussure made them and they are useful. Single letters recombined do not qualify as hypograms ((right away a kind of hierarchy presents itself, the hypogram valued above, more difficult to qualify for…)). Single letters recombined after the other ones drop out are ((only)) anagrams. Diphones make hypograms. So do triphones, multiphones; but not monophones, which make anagrams. Or "rien du tout," nothing at all, he writes in his notebook.

"Another manuscript which is supposedly kept in the Great Mosque of Tunis, but which is at present unavailable to us, one day perhaps will provide information with which we can further our studies." (Samuel Stern, *Les Chansons mozarabes*) His wistfulness.

The Story of the Jarcha, or where does this fit into the history of the Middle East according to our master narrative. These manuscripts of 11th, 12th and 13th century writing from Al-Andalus, the south of Spain, particularly Cordova and Seville, had been carried all over the Mediterranean during "the expulsion," during the Christian conquest. Stern knows of some that are kept in Tunis but he is not permitted to see them. Some were carried to Egypt and Palestine by fleeing Jews and Arabs. Since there was an interdiction prohibiting the destruction of writing, these pages, eventually not considered worth keeping, had been buried in sand. Thus they were preserved.

After WWII some were discovered in Egypt. They presented an incomprehensible text. In the early 1950s, Stern and other philologists began to make inroads after discovering that they were written in "merged" languages: Arabic, Hebrew, Romance (Proto-Spanish). Here were the combinations, generated by a "matrix of enunciation," or "assembly of enunciation"—the distillation of lyric in its essential public, social function. The themes, love, praise, wine, etc., "set" into the voice of an other, a deliberate "I am not the poet" I, the proposed capital O Other, mostly or always set by a male poet into the female voice, a constructed female scaffold of enunciation. Or a drunk. Or a dove.

In vernacular, the *jarcha*, the appendage or tail, distinguished from the classical language of the body, the main text, the *moaxaja* to which it was appended.

"Brulante," "burning like naphtha, like hot coals, like the talk of... artists" (from the 12th century treatise of the Egyptian writer Ibn Sana'al-Malk)

Esteban Pujals sends me Emilio Gomez Garcia's book, a Xerox of the Spanish text of the at present most complete collection of the *jarcha*, from Malaga, where he teaches, and I pretend to be able to read it, reading towards Jerusalem.

There are separate languages. We believe in them.

Quote from the questionnaire, it says here.

> • Which is the networked implication of supplementing new
>   thoughts with the same words?
> • What conveys a line like 'silence notes its own misreading'?

It is not known whether this questionnaire, devised by a Spanish teacher and publisher, was first written in Spanish and then translated by himself into English or written directly by him in English. The vocabulary is English, the "sentence melody" is not. Is the genotext, the engendering bloody struggle in the receptacle, languagized? culturized? Or does that happen during the differentiating warping and wefting that choosing words is?

The text that is presented is the enactment of two language experiences become one. Fusion. Verging and blending, postbinary blurring of overcoded infrastructure.

> Then there is sentence melody; they sing your language before
> any "language," any "message," any "content."
>   —Rachel Blau DuPlessis, *The Pink Guitar*
> . . . by the advent of a semiotic rhythm that no system of
> linguistic communication has yet been able to assimilate.
>   —Julia Kristeva, *Desire in Language*

Contact before content.

Do you "come upon" a thought? Do you take it as you find it? Frege, in his *Logical Investigations*, has us suppose that "a sentence is written on paper," and then that the "paper is cut up with scissors, so that on each scrap of paper there stands the expression for part of a thought."

Or bury the scraps in sand to preserve/hide them. And if they had never been found. If the interdiction had not been respected and followed "to the letter." Would these poems in an amalgam of language and tradition, making an entirely new thing, would this new thing still have come to exist in some form?

Without understanding or even hearing the words, you can recognize, for example, the language of leavetaking. This is real. If it exists before or beside or in the holding tank do we call it transcendence?

And then what is referred to as the "foreignness" in one's own—as if we own it—language, the basic condition, a baseline irritation. Communication occurred. Then the theory that constructs the official language, the process of regularization, occurred. There are conventions of use specific to time and place and other factors. Language is learned within a set of conventions. Then there is poetic language....

The translator takes a measure of the difference, takes a reading of the normative/non-normative relations in the written text, in the phenotext, the actual given on-the-page. The *differentia specifica* of "verbal art" is in its "set towards the message" qua message (Jakobson). Ordinary language minus social constraints equals poetic language (Kristeva).

The agreement.

The understatement.

"Society was now based on complicity in the common crime." (Freud, *Totem and Taboo*)

Whatever this common crime is, past or hidden, the common language, used by agreement, becomes convention, and means repression and a kind of safety. Safety from being challenged. The social pact of language becomes a law of silence. Excess, the unstructured, the unaccounted for, the rebellious, the delinquent is a threat. To control.

The well-known essay by Roman Jakobson about, primarily, Mayakovsky and Khlebnikov, is sometimes called, in English, "The Generation That Squandered Its Poets." In Kristeva's *Desire*, however, it has been translated as "The Generation That Wasted Its Poets" (translators Tom Gora and Alice Jardine). Here the origins of "waste" explode to the foreground: besides "to use unprofitably," or "to use without adequate return," we hear "to ravage, to lay waste, to destroy." These poets were not merely scattered or used carelessly, recklessly, as squander implies and says. They were "hit," "knocked off." They wore their colors. They were wasted.

Kristeva's theory becomes method when she identifies two opposing factions: society, the one that "wastes" its poets, artists, "in order to reproduce itself," and then the "we" who are "with" those whom society wastes in order to reproduce itself.

> Murder, death and unchanging society represent the inability to hear and understand the signifier as such—as ciphering, as a presence that precedes the signification of object or emotion.... The poet is put to death because he wants to turn rhythm into a dominant element....
>
> —*Ibid.*

The signifier exceeds the signified.
The text has more trying to push through
than what it simply points to.
This is surplus or waste.
I.e. what's most difficult to address in making translation.

> One cannot then, the argument would run, begin by identifying the meanings which language produces and use this as a normative concept to govern one's analysis, for the salient fact about language is that its modes of producing meaning are unbounded and the poet exceeds any normative limits. However broad the spectrum of possibilities on which one bases an analysis, it is always possible to go beyond them; the organization of words in configurations which resist received methods of reading forces one to experiment and to bring into play new types of relations from language's infinite set of possibilities....
>
> —Jonathan Culler, *Structuralist Poetics*

Culler presents a passage from Mallarmé, with translation:

> les mots, d'eux-mêmes, s'exaltent...

> the words of their own accord become exalted jewels...

The passage continues. The translator is unable to "resist received methods of reading" and interprets Mallarmé's lithe dazzle in terms of a flattened, normative reading, retro, dead in the water. He cannot go into the beyond, into the territory of Mallarmé's desire. Waste not, want not: no excess, no surplus, no mess: no desire equals stasis.
The poet wants to free the sign from denotation and does. The word is released from confinement of denotation, and not arbitrarily— motivated by this "other thing," this rhythmic thing.

There is a characteristic syntactic sound of, say, a political scientist, that is recognizable as such when he reads from his work, or when you read his work, regardless of the individual words and their semantic identities, histories. The texture of political science is a learned thing, a template through which drives, semiotic choric matter, what-have-you would be hard-pressed to pass.

Since poetry resists such received codes, it becomes the locus of "the struggle between rhythm and the sign system." (Kristeva) This states and locates a version of the central violence of language.

Plato resisted setting spoken language into writing because it would no longer be fluid, it would be fixed. This is how we know Plato to be a poet. What Plato put off discussing was the ability of the written language to question itself, albeit in terms of itself, in metalinguistic terms; even so to put itself at risk before the accusatory social and political machine.

If writing things down runs the risk of "fixing" them, making them rigidified, petrified, translating runs a multiple risk, where fix means pin down, often pinning down meaning at the expense of the writing; and then repairing things that might have been expressed innovatively or unconventionally. Renovate that poem so it will be clear, and if it is not clear, smoothed out, we-the-reader may say that it "reads like a translation." If it is not "the same," that is because the translator has chosen a nine for a ten. Brilliance beyond explanation. Great confusion at this point about what might be considered non-normative. The symbolic order as a kind of survival mechanism, establishing difference, turning its back on desire, which always and forever takes it by surprise.

> *genos*   offspring, EMERGING
> *phenon*   shining, CLARIFYING
> *typos*   the blow, the impression

We cannot get away from the violence. But we are now in the post-human. The photo in *Newsweek* (casually?) of a Haitian child eating a burnt morsel of Tonton Macoute.

> It is my design to render it manifest that no one point in its composition is referable to accident or intuition, that the work proceeded, step by step to its completion with the precise and rigid consequence of a mathematical problem.—*Edgar Allan Poe*

An unprecedented word order makes us ponder over the materiality of the words themselves, and any meaning we may come up with will be inseparable from the physical

arrangement of the words. For it is precisely in the originality
with which words have been placed in relation to one another
that we immediately recognize the poetic specificity of
Mallarmé's language: it is the poetic message.—*Leo Bersani*
Consider that Mallarmé, as well as Baudelaire, was a translator of Poe's
work.

> Caught from some unhappy master who unmerciful
>   Disaster
> Followed fast and followed faster till his songs one

> burden bore—
> Till the dirges of his Hope that melancholy burden bore
>   Of 'Never—nevermore.'
> > —*Poe, from "The Raven"*

.... Quelque maitre malheureux à qui l'inexorable Fatalité a
donné une chasse acharnée, toujours plus acharnée, jusqu'à
ce que les chants n'aient plus qu'un unique refrain, jusqu'à
ce que les chants funèbres de son Espérance aient adopté ce
mélancolique refrain: "Jamais! Jamais plus!"
> —*Baudelaire's translation of the above passage*

...pris à quelque malheureux maitre que l'impitoyable Désastre
suivit de près et de très près, suivit jusqu'à ce que ses chansons
comportassent un unique refrain; jusqu'à ce que les chants
funèbres de son Espérance comportassent le mélancolique
refrain de "Jamais—jamais plus."
> —*Mallarmé's translation of the same passage*

Say you could calculate it, the impact of the combinations. One
calculation per register. And then perform the substitutions: one for
each calculation of the sum of the registers, an equivalent. Register by
register, or by totals? Factor in memory, history, operating as a drive,
as impulse, but prethetic, as precondition for the thetic. Engendering
is eventually reduced to a choice, articulation occurs in terms of the
choices.

The choice comes out of all possibilities.

"All possibilities" is another name for semiotic *chora*. *Chora* presents
them all, then the other registers come to recognize. *Chora* continues
to shove up against the thetic shield, the condensation of possibilities.
Chora tries to break through, whence the charge, urgency.

Choice of one, pressure of the rest.

(*He opens a tome and begins.*)
It says: "In the beginning was the Word."
Already I am stopped. It seems absurd.
The *Word* does not deserve the highest prize,
I must translate it otherwise
If I am well inspired and not blind.
It says: In the beginning was the *Mind.*
Ponder that first line, wait and see,
Lest you should write too hastily.
Is mind the all creating source?
It ought to say: In the beginning there was Force.
Yet something warns me as I grasp the pen,
That my translation must be changed again.
The spirit helps me. Now it is exact.
I write: In the beginning was the *Act.*
                    —*Goethe, from "Faust," trans. Walter Kaufman*
Force, *Kraft,* Hegelian negativity.
Τριτον...τη χωρας
        ...thirdly, the receptacle, now called space
        ...
        ...space, which is eternal and indestructible, which provides
        a position for everything that comes to be and which is
        apprehended without the senses by a kind of spurious
        reasoning and so is hard to believe in.
                    —*Plato, "Timaeus," trans. Desmond Lee*
(It is still hard to believe in, but perhaps the current model for this type
of faith can be found in theoretical physics.)
        we look at it indeed in a kind of dream and say that everything
        that exists must be somewhere and occupy some space, and
        that what is nowhere
(What is nowhere?)
        and that what is nowhere in heaven or earth is nothing at all.
        And because of this dream state
(that writing sometimes is)
        we are not awake to the distinctions we have drawn and others
        akin to them, and fail to state the truth about the true and
        unsleeping reality.—*Ibid.*
Here is part of that last sentence translated by Reverend Bury:

…we are unable also on waking to distinguish clearly the unsleeping and truly subsisting substance, owing to our dreamy condition, or to state the truth….

In truth I was dreaming about having all these pages of notes in my hand but not remembering anything about what was in them, and that the red sweater I wore overtop the yellow one was full of holes.

…the geno-text can be thought of as a device containing the whole historical evolution of language and the various signifying practices it can bear. The possibilities of all language of the past, present and future are given there, before being masked or repressed in the pheno-text.

—*Kristeva, Semiotike*

A system is a kind of damnation pushing us to perpetual abjuration; it is always necessary to make up another one, and that tiredness is cruel punishment.

—*Baudelaire, "Crime and Punishment"*

The young deaf man called Idelfonso in Susan Schaller's fascinating account, *A Man Without Words*, copied the movements and gestures of American Sign Language, as he saw it practiced, but with no inkling that these signs *signified*. (Is this *his* sentence melody? Or true materiality of the sign as object not function?) He had to sign for it. He did not understand "sign for." "Sign for it." He had (at least for the first 60 pages of his life, the first 26 years of this book) never entered the Symbolic Order. It seems truly astounding that at this moment there exists sufficient agreement that we can refer to a Symbolic Order at all…. Symbols exist by agreement if not consensus. Idelfonso acquired these movements belonging to others, but for him they were not signs, they were truly arbitrary. His symbolic order was a magical language of one, in which meaning was specifically generated by and belonged to, referred back to, his own particular experiences. Green elicited a fear response from him, and so on. The manipulation of numbers—since they refer to themselves?—came much more easily and quickly than the connection between sign and referent.

In a way, translating is writing without memory, stealing another's memory. Is this the crime?

The advantage.

This is not appropriation but incorporation, the bloody struggle. Not avoidance. Entrapment, perjury. Ultimately, cannibalism.

Playing the disadvantage: an escape to writing

and a relief

and confinement (remember when confinement meant birthing?):
shackled back to back to the other, and our lifetimes are not congruent.
"We've known each other for so long now."
Try to dare to tell it.
The grand intrusion. There is no social space between: there is, however,
an irreparable fault. Is this the crime?
"The author is saying that...."
This is not translation, this is the *New York Times* book reviewer
explaining the book to you in a way designed to let you know you want
to buy it. ("What Mr. Ellis is evidently trying to say is that Patrick
Bateman lives in a morally flat world" etc.)

> Absolute speed, which makes us perceive everything at the same
> time, can be characteristic of slowness, or even of immobility.
> Immanence. It is exactly the opposite of development, where
> the transcendent principle which determines and structures
> it never appears directly on its own account, in perceptible
> relation with a process, a becoming.
> —*Claire Parnet, from Dialogues,*

a blended account of a conversation between her and Gilles Deleuze. In
fact, an account of "the between."
At first I didn't know how to read that second set of relationships: did
the "it" of "It is exactly the opposite of development" belong with the
following subordinate clause beginning "where?" Or was the "where"
referring to "development," its opposite? The opposite of absolute speed,
that is.
This seems to propose development as an alternative to the Platonic
dreamspace, the Receptacle, the Enclosure-without-bounds. Out of
bounds. What is out of bounds depends on who's the referee. Who
calls it.
A bloody encounter.
"thought's reason"
thème (Fr.) translating from the mother tongue, or native language, *into*
a foreign language
version (Fr.) translating from the foreign tongue into the native language
Finally,
in the last book of the *Aeneid* a treaty is made. It has been known for
a long time that the newcomers, the Trojans, having escaped the fiery
destruction of their city, have come to live their fate, found the new

city, here. The indigenous people have been fighting this fate, these
attackers, and they are losing, so they make a truce. The terms of their
agreement: Aeneas can marry Lavinia, the king's daughter, and will
take over as ruler, but the indigenous people will keep their name and
their language. "The people" is inseparable from their language. The last
aside: elsewhere in the *Aeneid*, Nisus to Euryalus, or was it the other
way round? "Is it the gods who give us these divine orders or is it we
who make our ideas into gods?"

Coleridge asks, "If you take from Virgil his diction and his meter, what
do you leave him?"

"Transcendental signified" could be that the signified is transcendental
or that the transcendental is signified, the difference being in the
direction of the action, of our understanding of the action.

In medieval terms, translation was the transfer of an empire. Later it
referred to a transferral of learning from one center, say Athens, to
another, such as Paris.

Social and political stasis and calcification are represented by and are a
function of the code's fear of and refusal of the surplus of signification,
the thing that moves, that breathes, that pivots, that makes rhythm, the
message that moves like revolution kept outside the palace gates by the
text, the telos, manageable, managed, ordered by syntax, semantically
controlled by convention of the symbolic order. The space exceeds the
container, constantly threatening to spill over. The overdetermined text
bears witness to the struggle.

It is easy to see how translation runs the risk of being doubly
overdetermined.

Delivered as part of a panel on translation
at the Kootenay School of Writing
Vancouver, 1991
Published in *Raddle Moon* (#11, 1992)

IN THE TIME OF PROSODY

In the time of imagination, prosody becomes the reference system, the set of locating coordinates. In the time of prosody, imagination becomes the realm. In the imagination of time, prosody is memory. In a poetry of thought, memory, time and imagination, the tracking impulses are multifarious. Mrs. Carlyle's response to Robert Browning's "Sordello," that she could not make out whether Sordello was a man, a city or a book, recast into assertion rather than skepticism, or at least into speculation, becomes strikingly apt as a description of a particular strand of contemporary poetry. In the imagination of this time and place, prosody becomes the foundations, bearing memory and history and experience in its continuity and breath, breadth and measure.

"she forgets to leave off reading"

One writes in order to leave off reading. One writes it down in order to read. One writes it down variously as it is variously true, true in the sense of coexisting, present even when absent in the act of being recalled or remembered.

"I find phrases in your poems and letters that are so very much enough in themselves" (Alec Finlay, Morning Star Publications, Edinburgh, letter, 26 January 1994)

But the phrases that strike Alec Finlay, reader/editor, as being apt for his Folio project do not exist, do not *come into existence* in a vacuum, on their own. They are points along the way, and they are single threads that gain their strength through having been spun and woven in, with other threads, to create a pattern (a woman, a city, a book), a texture, a text. That is their logic, that is their story, for they are part of a story, they belong to it; they long for it if they are separated out. And this longing can have value in itself, is discovery, or might be.

Introductory Remarks,
Browning Society, San Francisco
4 February 1994

A MINIMUM OF MATTER

Notes on Robin Blaser, "The Fire," and "The Moth Poem"

For after all, sure as it is that I see my table, that my vision terminates in it, that it holds and stops my gaze with its insurmountable density, as sure even as it is that when, seated before my table, I think of the Pont de la Concorde, I am not then in my thoughts but am at the Pont de la Concorde, and finally sure as it is that at the horizon of all these visions or quasi-visions it is the world itself I inhabit, the natural world and the historical world, with all the human traces of which it is made—still as soon as I attend to it this conviction is just as strongly contested, by the very fact that this vision is mine.
Maurice Merleau-Ponty, *The Visible and the Invisible*.
(tr. Alfonso Lingis, Northwestern University Press, Evanston, 1968)

———

I desired sunrise to revise itself as apparition…
Barbara Guest, *Fair Realism* (Sun & Moon, Los Angeles 1989)

———

As things seen and heard are not *there*, these same things shimmer, flicker in the heat of the "what is at stake" here. How does *auto-da-fé* shift between declaration of faith and the sentence to be burned alive at the stake?

Robin Blaser's "The Fire" is dedicated "especially to Ebbe Borregard," and was written for an occasion, "for a few in San Francisco, where I read it last March 8th." We may read it in *The Poetics of the New American Poetry*, eds. Donald Allen & Warren Tallman, Grove Press, 1973; or in *Caterpillar 12*, July 1970, ed. Clayton Eshleman, a special issue devoted to Robin Blaser and Jack Spicer, indicating a prior "last March 8th"; or possibly in *Pacific Nation #2*, 1968, referring to an even earlier March 8th.

"The Fire" begins with the introduction of the invisibility of the crucial. It goes on to privilege image as representation of this invisible crucial,

to value image above concept or idea, and to propose the possibility
or desirability of "holding" or "catching" this invisibility in a line "by
sound and heat," ultimate ultrasound, shaping… what is at stake here,
flowers of salt all around. The eidetic diegesis: "I'm haunted by a sense
of the invisibility of everything that comes into me (aware that nothing
is more invisible than emotion—by emotion, I mean the heat of one's
sense of the war, or a place, or a body, or of the extensions of these,
the earth, the existence of gods, and so forth—the I-have-seen-what-I-
have-seen, recorded by Pound in Canto II)." (Blaser, "The Fire") *Seen.
Recorded. Desired.* In what order?

1968 also saw publication of Robert Duncan's *Bending the Bow*, from
New Directions, the "Introduction" a crisis that coheres, beginning with
"The War." The culmination of this critical turbulence is "Articulations,"
itself beginning with Dante and exploding "our composure" with its
announcement of "the Satanic person of a President," sparking the
subsequent charges of "Passages 13 The Fire":
    Hell breaks out an opposing music.
this other fire ignited by
      …those who would be Great Nations Great Evils.

The heat or affinity of these conflagrations evokes, by the negation
of the negation, the shape—elusive—of something that in 1990 will
come to be invoked as *La communità che viene, The Coming Community*
(Giorgio Agamben, tr. Michael Hardt, Einaudi: Turin 1990; University
of Minnesota Press, Minneapolis 1993): "What the State cannot
tolerate in any way, however, is that the singularities form a community
without affirming an identity (Cities were imaginary—like oceans. The
name of a man would be a town. (Blaser, "The Fire")), that human
beings co-belong without any representable condition of belonging.…"

In "The Medium," the relationship between its musicality and the
tempering of others' scales, as well as the narrative of the timing,
are perceptible here in or as "a darkness," a rhythm reflecting its
"reluctance." In another matrix or in other verbal conjunctions this
would not or does not occur, would not be obvious. And yet once
posited it is not cagey or even subtle but direct and immediate, the
"something" of experience. There seems to be another speech back
of this speech. "The Medium" scores emotion inchoate in "invisible

pencil," on Blaser's table as "Atlantis / draws back from the shine on the water," from Atlantis to water a precision, a meticulousness of microtonal attention, anticipating the flow of a/the *next* line where "the crumbling pieces flow unattached." And then, you have to trust that someone on the other side of the *"pure transparency"* will not flip the switch, locking you in, or was it under? A rocking motion is a kind of compass.

The spotlight generated by rhythm or ideology posits speculation about the relationship between rhythm and ideology, "heard, seen and spun," a question for the millenial turn at hand. Odysseus is space man, Penelope the figure of time itself. Now we are in imagined memory, Atlantis, moth-time.

Where, so to speak, a public language has closed itself in order to hold a meaning, it becomes less than the composition of meaning. It stops and relegates both the language and its hold on the "real" to the past. The place of language in the social, as performance of the "real," is displaced to a transparency and becomes an imposition rather than a disclosure. Robin Blaser, "Statement," *The New Long Poem Anthology* (ed. Sharon Thesen. Coach House Press, Toronto 1991)

The safety of a closed language is gone and its tendency to reduce thought to a reasonableness and definiteness is disturbed. "The Practice of Outside, an essay by Robin Blaser," *The Collected Books of Jack Spicer* (ed. Robin Blaser. Black Sparrow Press, Santa Barbara 1975)

Distance is non-metrical, that is, not exactly measurable, spinning in the multiple readings of (e)motion from "cloud" to "crowd." ("Paradise Quotations") Every paradise hovers in this little distance. "From the Marysville Buttes a cut / northeast, up lava flows / towards Paradise— not that city / but the Single One / of all our meeting...." (Kenneth Irby, "Fragments," *Caterpillar 10*, January 1970). In this same issue of *Caterpillar* can be found eight poems from *The Holy Forest*. Except for "The Translator: A Tale," from *The Moth Poem* (1962-1964), all are from *Charms* (1964-1968).

The image develops *in static*. The static is motion generated by the image or arising spontaneously between the image and its reader. "it, it, it, it," the "unexpected myth," the paste imitation which is also the real jewel, locked up in a vault, out of sight. Neither perception nor possession is the poetry. The undefended eye, that is, the open eye catches, is caught by words, that is, by air. Its rhythm is a mirror simultaneously reflecting and deflecting. Like a song, or words displaced in a dream, it appears to be heard, it disappears. Prosody speaks with some authority, as the shape of "*the white rose of Eddyfoam*" persists through time.

"The Supper Guest" arrives in a "minimum of matter" (Merleau-Ponty) and an "infinitely small vocabulary" (Spicer). "I love waits with cold wings furled…," said HD. As though the Nerval translations already inhabited these rooms, the music is familiar yet unrecognizable, words anticipate themselves, "a gift, a promise of a debt." ("Salut") According to its own concordant logic, the instrument has a blind spot, this "language a darkness." In deference to this darkness itself, we separate in silence.

I have found in the serial poem a way to work from my displaced, uncentered 'I' in order to be found among things—relational, at least to what I can. Recent theory tells us writers that the author is gone from his/her authority. That seemed real enough before theory ever hit home. And, without authority, a conversation went on… so, I guess "The Moth Poem, "though back there, is still working at my initial sense of the multiplicity of times, persons, gods, things, thoughts, places, and stuff—folding—
Robin Blaser, *The New Long Poem Anthology*, "Statements"

Poetry the true fiction
Barbara Guest, *Fair Realism*

PG: Obviously part of the joy is that it's bigger than you are.
MP: Certainly.
PG: And it works because one keeps reading back into it, one keeps finding oneself in that figure.
MP: And maybe that becomes a figure of itself, for that idea of imaginary community in which poets tend to dwell with others. Not to say that it's outside the real, but it's constructed through the imagination and sometimes

*in opposition to the principles of reality that are laid on us, all of which say
'you should not be doing this.'*
"Interview with Michael Palmer," Peter Gizzi, *Exact Change Yearbook*
1995

*Deeper—there is the defense of longing for love against the practice of
love.... But the work is solitary, and seen thus: one has strength in the
solitude that takes the place of loneliness for solitude is within the practice of
love. The mute entrance towards fulfillment.*
Robert Duncan, letter to Robin Blaser, 28 February 1959

Citation is invocation, cross-referenced. The "imaginary community,"
or "community to come," never at hand, pregnant with contradiction,
has its points of agreement; unavoidable tautology, since it is defined
by its points of agreement. Time and space are conventions that exist
in relation to such points of agreement. Loss, the uncompromised
"solitary," provides the bottom line, reading uncalibrated memory.
There is no "general view" of experience; perhaps the promise of "the
non-invasive association of memory" (Michael Emre, conversation).

At which point we agree enough to speak about how something is
made, as though blood flows through rope, blew through a rope.
Context can promote citation as authority, legitimacy; desire can mark
it as the celebration of companionship, proofing faith, proving the
being among. Its agency is felt reality, its work fiery apprehension.

"The world, like every in-between, relates and separates..." (Hannah
Arendt, *The Human Condition*) also reads as "The work, like every
in-between, relates and separates...." "An emphasis falls on reality."
(Barbara Guest, *Fair Realism*) Which challenges a prevailing tide
not merely consisting of forgetfulness but of the violent refusal of
complexity in the name of stylish variety, the refusal of form (whether it
involve history, context, a figure and ground relationship) in the name
of the "random violence" playing over or behind or around us.

But "the near object and the far object are not comparable."
(Merleau-Ponty)

a song}   —think about
I made}   space *drawn* by syntax i.e.
a coat}   delivered in the tensions and questions
                      of syntax

What is *agreement* (north) held up against (measured? against?)
convention (North)? We are north of you, or the eight-ply of the heavens
are all folded into one darkness North of you…. "Need" does not
arise from "things". Remembering (*mnesia*, from *mneson*, mindfulness)
and the need to speak arise from the absence of…as departure is a
prerequisite for any arrival.

our articulations, our
                    measures.
It is the joy that exceeds pleasure.
Robert Duncan, "The Dance," *The Opening of the Field* (New Directions
1960)

…—what I love about poetry is the astonishment of language— its
surprising abilities—that poetry guards the materiality of language—its
workability—its careful steps….
Robin Blaser, "Hello," *Sulfur 37*

Shocking greeting, "you, priest, must know why you strike" ("Salut")
easily misreads as, rhymes with, "you, priest, must know why you
write," a reading-into-assertion foregrounding the reversal ever present
in statement. Unexpectedly flipping the reader's "statement" into (the
reader's?) "question," image re-establishes its right to represent faith
bursting into flames.

The actual fire has raged around the crystal. The crystalline poetry to be
projected, must of necessity, have that fire in it. You will find fire in The
Walls Do Not Fall, Tribute to the Angels, *and* The Flowering of the
Rod. *(15 Dec. 1949)*
But The Walls Do Not Fall *is, in a sense, like certain passages of* The Gift,
runic, divinatory. This is not the "crystalline" poetry that my early critics
would insist on. It is no pillar of salt nor yet of hewn rock-crystal. It is the
pillar of fire by night, the pillar of cloud by day. It is divinatory, I say, for it
seems to indicate, even to predict that Cloud of Witnesses, the starry cloud or

star-nebula, as I later call the group of young RAF pilots: John, Lad, Larry,
Ralph and Charles tap out their message, with (as one of them spelt clearly
on the table) o-t-h-e-r-s m-a-n-y. (Dec. 30, 1949)
This was an actual experience:
> *he stands by my desk*
> *in the dark*
(Jan. 5, 1950) "HD by *Delia Alton* (Notes on Recent Writing)," HD
(*The Iowa Review* Fall 1986)

And full of contradictions. Book of images, present like any permanent,
elusive event. *Elusive*: On the way (via the *OED*) to "elusive" we run
across "dogstones," and note that this is the name for various species of
British Orchis, "from the shape of the tubers."

Elusive: from the Latin ppl. stem *elus-* of *eludere*, to elude, *e-* (out) +
ludere (to play). Out of play, from play, a product of play; one obsolete
sense is "baffle" or "fool," "to disappoint. "

The music of this "obsolete" ex-ludic disappointment, baffling, inheres:
> *My Dear—*
>> *we end with you*
> *circling your garden...*
the circling continuing in downturning spiral, the vocalic {long i—long
e—short a} trajectory from the first words, "My Dear" to the final
"somebody else's idea" recapitulated in the final word, "idea."

Elusive: Another obsolete sense, to while away (tedium). 1660, R.
Coke, *Justice Vind.* "Men seek... company to divert themselves, so to
elude the length of time." To escape by dexterity or stratagem (a blow,
attack, danger, or difficulty); to evade the force (of an argument; to
evade compliance with or fulfillment of (a law, order, demand, request,
obligation, etc.); to slip away from, escape adroitly from (a person's
grasp or pursuit, *lit.* and *fig.*) (How to distinguish *lit.* from *fig.*?) Milton,
Paradise Lost, ix, 158, "Of these (the flaming Ministers) the vigilance
/ I dread, and to elude, thus wrapt in mist / Of midnight vapour glide
obscure...." Of things, to elude inquiry, notice, observation, etc. To
remain undiscovered or unexplained. 1878, Tait & Stewart, *Unseen*
Universe vi, §177, "So infinitesimally small as to elude our observation."

With assiduous application to "O-t-h-e-r-s / m-a-n-y" reading through things, to build through-composed or clear-composed work, without device as safety net; but, rather, to be startled by form's dynamic insistence.

I looked at my paper and suddenly I saw that the, all the music, was already there. John Cage, notes for "Daughters of the Lonesome Isle"

The accidental vision becomes the incident "How to follow the gaze that stares into its future-past?" is just a question, like "Where is the country with the all-night bookstores?" Realism is a character that believes in… us? Is it fair in the sense of just? Or just beautiful in and for itself, because we say so? Poetry believes in reality and references the investigatory philosophy of the crisis of "the destruction of experience" (Agamben), always having anticipated it. Not only is reality's visibility in question, so is its name, "emotion." We call it "emotion," or sometimes "experience." Is it, then, outside experience? Or only in the possession of the specificity of "having one"?

I have worked since 1955 to find a line which will hold what I see and hear, and which will tie a reader to the poems, not to me. RB, "The Fire"

The idea of the moth's or the poem's resistance to "being seen," or caught: The generative nature of this resistance: The resistance of the image to being seen generates the poem. Fair realism eludes its image as the elusive image is being sung. "It is essentially reluctance the language / a darkness, a friendship, tying to the real / but it is unreal." RB, "The Medium"

Even on Sunday: Essays, Readings, and Archival Materials
on the Poetry and Poetics of Robin Blaser,
ed. Miriam Nichols
(National Poetry Foundation, 2002)

"ERROR OF LOCATING EVENTS IN TIME"[1]

For Edmond Jabès

infinite series refusing reduction

"States where you dwell places of rumbling"[2]
(Anne-Marie Albiach, *État*)

The acid or etched plate, the impression of which is a portrait of all that is left of the attempt, the impression of evidence. Prosody's requisite number, quantity, a book on the pillow, impossible to remember, a boat on its side, impossible to forget, conventions of agreement crumbling, comfort gone, "comfort" remembered. Familiar words and old words reinvent the language. In every case the question arises whether to leave them fragments, or, adding and splicing, conform to discursive convention's declaratives; assertions complete in their own sense of themselves, authority of capitulation, the address: X, for moving outward, which might appear to be at the same time. Function defies definition, there is no center.

> The common behavior of mankind is the system of reference
> by means of which we interpret an unknown language.
> (Wittgenstein, *Philosophical Investigations*)

What would the departure from the assumptions of "the common behavior of mankind" be? And what bearing would that departure have on reference and on other factors relevant to the production of language? In the wake of experiencing the great travesty, (reading backwards) perversion of the myth of progress, came the desire to relocate in an outside *were there one*. But every exile is implicated in the *something* that Emmanuel Levinas might term "the there is," Edmond Jabès "the desert." And so the initiation to difference, the impulse to

---

[1] "Error of Locating Events in Time" is the title of a poem by Claude Royet-Journoud. It appeared in *Politiques de l'oubli,* and the first sections were included in the volume of tributes, *Pour Edmond Jabès.*
[2] Unless otherwise indicated, the translations are my own.

mark it, to *language* differently, to inscribe otherness and align the address from there, *là-bas*.

> This vertical habits our 'nape.' in fact we are walking let us believe it horizontally. absent from time. silent from motion. (Albiach, letter to Jean Daive)

> *human quotation marks* as from the trenches

If the common project were departure: at what distance do reason and imagination elide? We understand the proposition of book as place. Its time has no eventuality. In the tradition of questioning, in a writing which is continually unwriting itself, is the underwriting asking?

> …the discourse never begins, only repeats itself over and over. But the poet…. (Maurice Blanchot, "Mallarmé and Literary Space")

The connection between name and thing, relentlessly elusive, exists by tenuous agreement. Between name and name. What is it when "common behavior as a system of reference" is *désoeuvré*, undone, unworked, out-of-work? The ex-war-correspondent remarks, "They tell us about the smart bombs, but they're not saying anything about the dumb bombs." "What if they hadn't told us anything? What if there had been only silence?" she asked. This is one extreme, resistance proving new community.

Maurice Blanchot's text, "The Refusal," was published in the second issue of a magazine called *14 juillet*, in October 1958. His uncharacteristic explanatory footnote in *L'amitié*, where it was republished in 1971, explains that the text "was written a few days after General de Gaulle was returned to power, this time not by the resistance but by the mercenaries." "The Refusal" begins:

> At a certain moment, in the face of public events, we know that we must refuse. The refusal is absolute, categorical. No discussion, nor hearings of reasons. It is in what is silent and solitary even while affirming itself as it must in the light of day. The men who refuse and who are bound by the force

of refusal know that they are not yet together. The time of common affirmation has been taken away. What they have left is irreducible refusal, the friendship of this certain No, unshakable, rigorous, that binds them in solidarity.

And then, near the end of this short piece,

> When we refuse, we refuse by an action without malice, without elation, anonymously, as much as possible, for the power of refusal is not effected beginning with ourselves, nor in our single name, but starting from a very impoverished beginning that belongs at first to those who cannot speak.

The refusal to take the "desire for collectivity and fix it to a process of consumption" (Jerry Estrin, "Cold Heaven").

Convention affirms relations of power and of authority. The form of *The Book of Questions*, in its irritation, is a *dispersal* of authority and of the conventions of written power. Its form of questions, endless and beginningless, can be read as interview, formally linking Talmudic investigation with a contemporary device, the device often a structured refusal of conclusion. A-totalizing. The form is not ironic, does not depend upon the collusion underwriting irony. Nor is it history. History, in its teleology, has a responsibility all its own. Its stated objective is "to find out the truth." This is something to keep in mind.

Eros and truth.

"You could not understand what you were seeing," wrote Peace Corps administrator Norman Rush describing his experience of approaching piles of elephant dung in the middle of a road in Botswana. The reason you could not understand what you were seeing was that species of butterfly had colonized the piles of dung, one kind to a pile; so that each was characterized by a different color, fluttered and appeared to pulsate. Image is comfort: possibly it will recognize and locate us. We document our different truths.

"To find out the truth" was the given objective of *The Report of the Parliamentary Delegation* presented by the Prime Minister, First Lord

of the Treasury and Minister of Defence, to the British Parliament,
by command of His Majesty, April, 1945. The document to be sold
publicly for twopence net. From *Buchenwald Camp: The Report of a
Parliamentary Delegation* (henceforth referred to as "the report"):

> On 19th April, 1945, in the course of a statement in the House
> of Commons on the German concentration camps, the Prime
> Minister said:—
> I have this morning received an informal message from General
> Eisenhower saying that the new discoveries, particularly at
> Weimar, far surpass anything previously exposed. He invites
> me to send a body of Members of Parliament at once to his
> headquarters in order that they may themselves have ocular and
> first-hand proof of these atrocities. The matter is of urgency....
> The object of this visit is to find out the truth....

From the House of Lords: Earl Stanhope and Lord Addison; and from
the House of Commons (where no Jew was permitted to sit before the
mid-nineteenth century): Colonel Wickham, Sir Archibald Southby,
Mrs. Tate, Mr. Ness Edwards, Mr. Silverman, Mr. Graham White, Sir
Henry Morris-Jones, Mr. Driberg.

From the report:

> We left London by air on the afternoon of Friday, April 20th.
> We should like to pay tribute to the efficiency and care with
> which the arrangements for our flights were handled by the
> officers of the Transport Command and by the crews of the
> Dakotas in which we flew, etc.... On arrival in France (where
> we spent the Friday night), we were greeted and hospitably
> entertained by General Eisenhower and his staff. We proceeded
> by air to Weimar on the following morning, arriving at
> Buchenwald Camp at about 11 a.m. on Saturday, April 21st.

The report continues:

> Buchenwald Camp is set in hilly, well-wooded country about
> 15 minutes' drive from Weimar. It dates from 1934. It is badly
> laid out, on sloping, uneven ground. The walls and paths are

ill-kept; at the time of our visit they were covered with dust, which blew about in the wind, and in wet weather the camp must be deep in mud....

Over the main gate of the camp is the inscription "Recht oder Unrecht—Mein Vaterland" (my country, right or wrong).

Identity puts us in a state.

Over the entrance to one of the Jewish cemeteries in Toronto, Canada, is the inscription "House of the Living." Placing a pebble on the gravestone, a small stone atop a large one, is a gesture of standing-in-for, relationship, a substitution for the absence of being together, its comfort. A marker of the not-being-together, marking the cut. A word placed next to another word is this deliberate. We read what we "see," write what we "want" in the face of inexplicable information, irreparable loss, trauma: autisms enacted in writing as written gesture. Truth is the document's convention. What is silence, unfolding in time, or what is silence but time unfolding?

"This is not a book for you" (title of a text by Edmond Jabès published in an issue of *Action poétique* dedicated to the work of Claude Royet-Journoud). Jabès writes: "Bathed in silence, worked by this silence which is not exactly silence but last silent words, always last because heard after the others...." Silence heard after. Silence as substance, heard. What is absence but absence as substance, the condition of existence, or call it faith.... There are unnamable crossroads here, one for a point of meeting of oral and written language, and at least one for the point of departure from measured time.

From the *Book of Questions:* "And Yukel said: In a village in central Europe, the Nazis—one night they buried some of our brethren alive." (Scrupulously, the translator provides a variant, "one night they buried alive some of our brethren.") It's crumbling, hard to hold on to, resisting its location in time, in place. "I am searching for a kind of platitude" (Royet-Journoud, "A Craft of Ignorance", tr. J. Simas). "If one pushes the literal to its extreme, as Wittgenstein has done, one falls into terror."

The report is littered with objectives (reliability, intelligence, truth, etc.).

> One 14-year-old boy, Abraham Kirchenblat, originally of
> Radom, Poland, impressed members of our party as an
> intelligent and reliable witness; he stated that he had seen his
> 18-year-old brother shot dead and his parents taken away, he
> believed for cremation. He never saw them again.

In the report there are hyphens between the number and year, and
between year and old, for it is numbingly faithful. In the crematorium
was a row of capacious arched ovens, each still containing calcined ribs,
skulls and spinal columns.

> *the Object.*   in parentheses
> it executes
> attraction to the earth   The ground dissolves, it
> resolves the equation of the disparity   A step into....
>   (Albiach, *Mezza Voce*)

Insistence on the history inscribed into the individual words elicits
equally insistence upon their naked contextless ahistorical presence,
sense or function—unaccented—what is function without syntax,
without telos, answer, foregrounding of the temporal/atemporal axis:
work that can't be reduced to an advertising slogan or to a single
characteristic gesture: the thing or object *irreducibility*.

> *Do I have to prove to you what was shattered, dispersed like light?*

"Frequently the rabbis allowed themselves to indulge in farfetched
interpretations and narrations which were clearly intended to
delight the fancy as well as to instruct." (Midrash) Celebration of
the multiplicity of meaning, its indivisibility. Relativity is built in,
the questions themselves are the response. Unity is unassuming, the
interconnections (semes, morphs, combinant and recombinant) are
signs and structurers of continuity, *con*, with, telling along the way how
to be "read in with," or "into" the rest of the text which is its *con*text.

In regard to larger blocks of narrative material, the characteristic biblical
method for incorporating multiple perspectives appears to have been

not a fusion of views in a single utterance but a montage of viewpoints arranged in sequence.... (revolution in biblical Israel) left little margin for neat and confident views about God, the created world, history and man as a political animal or moral agent. ... (Robert Alter, *The Art of Biblical Narrative*)

Clear as day, the lapses are written in different ways, the form coincides completely with the address from the margins. Locating events in time localizes, contains and delimits. Do we crave a past? This address that involves and implicates the reader in the writing field and into its borderlands is a kind of affirmation "resistant to the specious authority of form." (Michael Palmer introducing Edmond Jabès, San Francisco 1983) To see it through has not the same objective as getting through it.

> in the dynamic of the dark, or in the darkening of this memory, in the present illusory optic, dwells only this 'blackness', frame that does not leave off deepening from and open cube whereby the engulfing or the gifting of the abyss reiterates from four (mortal meanwhile—) breathes us. The eye takes on the size of the body, no longer assessing it by number or measure in fiction, but the body vision sees the numbers come undone from it, in memory of the letter.
>
> isolated letter even though existing only in relation to meager trace of seeing that it matters in its very elaboration.— Such this image of thought, darkened and light, it concerns the point of reference: place, placement, and the time of the disintegration of light at the center (still illusory) varies with our positions. our reversals of situation in space also hardly linear:
>
> (Albiach, "LOI(E)", *Anawratha*)

What gravity—G spot—attracts language to place? Writing the distance, the absence, the measure, the gap or chasm, the drought or draught; writing backwards defies the impulse to define, to move towards an ending which is always *the end,* which, *in conclusion, would be a relief.*

the angle of incidence
instructs as though inadvertently
(Michel Couturier, "Ablative Absolute," *Siècle à mains* 1968)

The agent is language itself, its indomitability an uncertainty principle
enacting itself, an undoing of form or an undone form, thus another
definition of what form might be. What it foregrounds is the instant of
crystallization into language, liquid crystal, continuous and sudden in
appearance in the supersaturated void. The untenable tension between
rhythm and the infinite, the infinite present within each word, in every
letter, threatens the proposition of center, of certainty, of comfort. What
is between repetition and difference?

> *She was alive as long as she continued speaking.*

Possibility of comfort remembered. The interruption of that. The
restating of that. Isn't language, after all, the antidote to solitary
confinement? In this telling which is endless asking, we are ever more
aware or constantly aware of the finitude of language. To ask questions
is simply to assume a form of address which implies all forms of address
in the spiral "of being numerous."

System of outside from which no one knew what to expect. Its
tenderness as matrix, its impulse towards life, eros as presence, writing
as the impulse to "see it through" in a form that says throughout "I am
not master of this thing. I am a participant." Relocating in prosodic
time. "…the pure power of transfiguration…." (Blanchot, "The Myth
of Mallarmé")

> Reading: replaying the departure of being (Pascal Quignard,
> "The Reader")

> practical work: for we must know (Albiach, *État*)

Relocation in prosodic time places the poet. Where she must
remain.

Freedom is in the misreading. Reading is between the vocables. Freedom is in the reconstitution of memory; since at every step it translates us. (Jabès, *Book of Questions*)

Content is often extracted from Jabès' writing in the name of argument or comfort in order to indicate or "prove" his theological / atheological, mystical / non-mystical, Jewish/ planetary/ cosmic, and so on, position, in the name of the myth or fiction of "summary" conventional perseveration. "…the unity of the tower of Babel…" writes Jabès. "And yet my language is that which I acquired and perfected here." Near the end of the *Aeneid* the conquered people of Latium, giving in to their pre-ordained fate, surrender to the Trojans who have come to found Rome. The request of the conquered people is that they keep their language, their *name*. There is an underlying assumption of decency, of possibility. Community in the shared language, in name, its specificity. And when this coherence turns in on itself in order to question itself, there is the possibility of the cut, the caesura separating a past and a future, community from community. Assumptions are undone, connections unworked. "The land where I live is not the one to which my ancestors gave language." (Jabès)

There is the impulse to make a grand inventory, to apply "the superego of continuity" (Barthes), thereby always having available the information that determines which things are a part of the desirable machine and which are irrelevant. Useful or irrelevant. Then there is an impulse to declare the impossibility of such an inventory. The very letters separate totality from infinity.

> White decimal / at the edge of space /
> I have wandered / between refusal and insistance /
> looking on the ground / snowing / name undoes
> form / the thaw the avalanche / remaking the absence
> (Jean Daive, *Décimal blanche*)

> *Looking from a little distance undoes image.*

> the feeling of a word: how it
> makes words shiver
> (André du Bouchet, *Notes on Translation*)

There are two letters.
One: the signifying letter immortal thus already dead....
Two: the desired letter, scattered....
                              (Claude Richard, "The Postage Stamp")

Finding the word on the page begins procedure through the language of
thinking to the borders of the unthinkable, the unthought. Form takes
this questioning as assertion of opening, continuing. The continuing
vigilance of the work, or working vigilance, is what Emmanuel Levinas
equates with "Jewishness" in Jabès' writing. "Do you know that the end
point of the book is an eye, that it has no eyelid?" (Levinas quoting
Jabès) When asked where he would "place" Edmond Jabès in "writing
today," Levinas responded with a question, asking whether a writer has
a place. "Isn't he the one who 'loses his place'?" Levinas attributes Jabès'
writing with "syntactic decency": as words pour forth, fission occurs
as sense begins to decompose into unprotected space, an "intranuclear
field without images, without mirages, without wonder..." (Levinas).

        to write up against the wall...

    Does the question of language constitute the blind task
    of my whole undertaking?
                    (Royet-Journoud to Roger Laporte, *Letter from Symi*)

The error of locating events in time becomes easily the terror of locating
events in time, which then becomes the terror of not locating events in
time, as well as its shadow, the error of not locating events in time.

Apex of the M, no.1
Spring 1994

A FEW WORDS ABOUT MINA LOY

A version of aversion to the world, this turning away having to do with the material of the dialectic: the dialogic, the material of abstraction, the former material world, the perceivable world, the emotional itself always a sophistic proving ground, a running sore, the wound never to heal, internalized, converted to psychosexual symptoms until the torus reverses the internal to surface skin, rash of symptoms located outside, the constructed outside.

This is an example of the kind of abstraction/reduction Mina Loy refused in her work which could be characterized as anti-heroic and non-rhetorical in its directness. Actually, we can say what we like about it, since no one ever sees it, not the extent of it, we can't know its specificity, we never see it, the work, in its diversity. So it remains occulted, an idea of someone's *génie* or eccentricity.

⸺

San Francisco
19 January, 1993

Last month, at Royaumont (a cultural center located in a 12th century Cistercian abbey near Paris, site of conferences and translation seminars), Henri Deluy (poet, editor of *Action poétique,* and chef extraordinaire) asked me to send the magazine *if* (directed by Henry Deluy, Jean-Charles Depaule, Liliane Giraudon & Jean-Jacques Viton) a few words about Mina Loy, about what she "means to me" today, these days.

Today, what I have before my eyes are images of war. The second anniversary of "Desert Storm," it begins again, it goes on. In color on the screen, aerial bombing, military destinations? civic? On the bombs we see written messages, laconic, in mortal hand, messages which will never arrive at their addressee, "Saddam."

"MORALITY was invented as an excuse for murdering the neighbors." (*Last Lunar Baedeker*)

At this juncture, Mina Loy reappears before me exuding her formidable rage, embodied in the inexorable brutality of her writing. Ezra Pound has written, "In the verses of Marianne Moore I detect traces of emotion; in that of Mina Loy I detect no emotion whatsoever." He was wrong. That is, one wonders what his definition of emotion could have been.

Another's resolution is frequently incomprehensible to us, inexplicable in its muteness. Her contemporaries often confused the poet, Mina Loy, with the poems; the persons of the poem with the poet; "I" and "threewomen" etc. with the biography of Mina Loy.

> Fundamentally unreliable
> You leave others their initial strength
> Concentrating
> On stretching the theoretic elastic of your
> conceptions (*LLB*)

"Had a man written these poems, the town might have viewed them with comparative comfort."—Alfred Kreymborg

Inacceptable sharpness? Too strong? Too comfortless coming from a woman? Shocking! There have been readers who attributed this sharpness, this bluntness, to a lack of experience, of facility.

> The green man-battling—"You are too big—I must eat you.—"
> The city swallows him—
> The greenish man-stifling—"I am not at home in you—"
> The city spits him up—
> The greenish man—execrating a passing woman—"You are not
>   a man—" (*LLB*)

Legible here is the sexualization of the city, of the object, the world, the word, where "*IRONY is the death rattle of emotion*" (*LLB*). A writing that is immediate and distinct, its own reduction, thus impossible to reduce. An ever-stunning compactness, ever a challenge. Its words, its verses hurl forth, pitilessly tracking to the point of visibility the coordinates of a remarkable and surprising vision, deploying lexical choices and strategies of address in the service of a rare constraint: luminous *"threatening nakedness"*(*LLB*).

"Like all modern art, this art...makes a demand for a creative audience" (*LLB*). Loy's observations about Gertrude Stein's writing, above all her description of *"the complete aesthetic organization"* offering the reader *"unlimited latitude for personal response"* (*LLB*), might appear to apply equally to her own work.

20 January 1993

We have never seen the spectacle, the range of this work: her objects, her paintings, her writing. (This cannot be overemphasized.)

Today is "Inauguration Day" here, we get a new President and what else? According to "our correspondent in Baghdad," there is rejoicing, there are expectations of a new era.

"It is an old religion that put us in our places." (*LLB*)

Mina Loy: Woman and Poet
eds. Maeera Schreiber & Keith Tuma
(National Poetry Foundation, 1998)

"A Picture Book Without Pictures"

I could not see the steady red light of Mars last
night, nor the pulsing nor the twinkling of Antares
in Scorpio, close (relatively) in the northern
summer sky.

───

I read (pronounced 'red') myself to sleep, over and over to wake. The cyclical time created in the form referenced "everyday time" from a place outside it, an unstable stable point called "the Moon" or, in this case, "my friend the Moon." "The actual extension of the realm of storytelling in its full unsocial breadth is inconceivable without the most intimate interpenetration of these two archaic types (the one who goes away and the one who stays home)."[1]

The pages were fragments in a framework, makeshift as you like, fragments of story, fragments of description, one stayed home-away-from-home (wrote or drew or read), and the other one sailed across the silent sky, but both were identified with the single site, the book-object. That was where one could find them and have them as often as one liked. They never got used up. There was no indebtedness. It was outside "the social."

───

The conditions exist in their own right. All the tale presents is "the framework of my thought" in words and word-pictures to someone who lives alone and in a "double loneliness" when there are clouds, "for my hand and my tongue are tied." Thus the abdication of authorial presence in favor of an absence relating the words of a cool yet comforting presence, reflecting light, and night's reflections. The storyteller modestly declines to "give a new *Thousand and One Nights* in pictures; but this would be too tedious." Instead, a *Weltanschauung* points towards a poetics for thirty nights, and then the account breaks

---

[1] Walter Benjamin, "The Storyteller," *Illuminations,* trans. Harry Zohn. Schocken Books 1969

off, necessity reabsorbed, with the words, "At that moment, the master of the bear appeared."

There are no easy transitions to safeguard the reader from the impact or force of the pulse following the pulse, or the drop following the pulse. The following pulse is implicit. This telling, a string of possibilities and memories, inventions and observation, sometimes achieved, and sometimes not, keeps the unknown, leaves it unknown. The unknown is brought back in the silver seine of the Moon to the one whose "hand and eye are tied," as only it could have been, veiled, the *rem praesentem* in its shroud. Neither visible nor invisible, "the broken cast of a work never penned."[2]

What is transmissible experience is the form of this telling, the pattern, rhythm and motif—the return. Real experience—real variations of days of nights. Waking up in the day of night, at the window, looking into the matter of grammar. Looking over the Ganges, the Mountains of Atlas, a town in Germany, a spectral city beneath the Veronica's veil of the sea. Seeing into memory, into a story of the bloodied velvet in the throne room of the Louvre after the July Revolution, or into an inscription from the Koran, written in sand, directing a caravan outside Fez. The initial instruction is, "Sketch what I relate to you." And then there is a choice.

Possibility is in the choice of play, even as the actor "had deep feeling and loved art enthusiastically, but Art did not return his love." *He* chose his end. But in the time outside that story ending has always been irrelevant, a plaything, considered and repeated, a plaything. Possibility is rhythm, *potentiality,* "the Nile Group," "The Laocoön," *commedia dell'arte,* Tasso, the circus, the wheel, the dice cup. It is never finishing ending, but sometimes is obscured by clouds and then there is still silence and the void, no story, no end of story.

---

[2] Giorgio Agamben, *Infancy and History: The Destruction of Experience,* trans. Liz Heron. Verso 1993

There is an "I" that is syntactic, a grammatical entity, set in opposition to, or simply in relation to the *no one,* the *nobody.* As if I is a name and the other the nameless grammar, Blanchot's *neutre.*[3] Each Other. Could it be that anonymity or the neutral inheres to tone? To the address, rather than to the literal fact of nomination? One remembers the pre-assigned and the mis-aligned, the non-fit that was secondary even though it had already been recognized from without as primary, pinned, like a tail, on the donkey: The gender of the narrator is "unassigned." That is, the name of the pronoun, "he" in this case, functions as a provisional marker, no body was automatic. It is only later with pressure from taller people that models and response eliminate the *potential/improper* position, relegating the non-reading self to the abject or proper position. But this was a learned thing, not in the sound of this story, heard in spite of this story's sound.

> "Once upon a time she climbed up the building using the elements of the façade as a ladder. Almost immediately she was corrected, since she had inadvertently taken action in the wrong gender."
>
> From "Destitution: A Tale"
> NC, *My Bird Book* (Littoral Press 1991)

"Following the polar bird," evening by evening, the familiar speech of storytelling is not the same familiar speech of everyday life, of personal address even while the words are shared. How does this anonymity contain both specificity and inclusion? For it is used here to indicate not generality but excess. Was it in that moonlit room I began to read towards *La Vita Nuova, Le roman de Silence,* "Dante and the Lobster," *Watt, The Opening of the Field, La notion d'obstacle* and *It Then*? In that "Paper House" to write towards "Joker" and "Ruth," *Mars, Moira,* and "Destitution," *Desire & Its Double*?

---

[3] Maurice Blanchot, *L'Entretien infini.* Gallimard 1969

In a volume without illustrations—"self-illuminated"—with hard
covers, covers of dark blue cloth, almost midnight blue. The cloth of
the back cover is now separated from the board, wrinkled and faded. Its
damage is eloquent enough, unarguable evidence of its having survived
a flood, it, the book, the witness *at that time.*

The flood was in a cave. The book had been loaned to Claudine, a
young Belgian woman, tall and narrow with fluffy brown hair, who
lived in this cave, her apartment, in the French sense of *cave,* basement,
a basement under a house built of local stone, attached to other similar
houses on both sides, its backside partially hewn into the rock wall
of the Alpes-Maritimes, in the same small walled village, dating from
medieval times, built upon Ligurian ruins, where I was living *at that
time,* in a former donkey stable. Claudine wore small round glasses
and, often enough, a plaid skirt, and she was the source of fascination
for a Canadian filmmaker, also on an extended visit to the village, who
at that time involved her in one of his projects, along with Mac, a Scot
who also frequently was to be seen walking through the village in his
plaid kilt. Little did we know *at that time,* that this same filmmaker
would one day return to the south of France to preside over the jury at
the Cannes film festival, while I, the owner of the blue and wet book,
would be living in the Bay Area.
Claudine's cave had one entrance, its single source of light, the front
door. As it happens, during the rainy season, the long gray winter (I was
told *at that time,* by another woman named Mimi, a Californian living
in the village *at that time,* that the climate was very similar to that of
"the Bay Area"), the water's access greatly exceeded that of the light of
day, and one day the cave flooded. Most of Claudine's belongings were
drenched. She saved the book, and returned it, still damp, with profuse
and unnecessary apologies.
The book, so the book is not illustrated yet is thus illuminated.

> I must have been given it soon after its publication in 1957,
> with its introduction by Auden, its smooth navy covers, no
> dust jacket, no words to disturb the infinite dark blue. The
> spine has a broad horizontal maroon stripe bearing the title in
> gilt letters now dull, in places almost erased by use. The paper
> is thin and at the same time pulpy, like newspaper. In memory

it appears a bigger book and heavier, as it would to a child of seven. I have no recollection of the actual moment of the gift.

Regarding the unbroken blue of the cover, I was misremembering. The book is now upon my desk, face up. On its "infinite dark blue" cover is a small cartouche, blood red or maroon, like the band on its spine. Inside it is stamped a small figure, a gilt runner carrying aloft a lighted torch. The band on the spine bears this same runner, contained, iconic rather than illustrative.

The actual title is *Tales of Grimm and Andersen: Selected by Frederick Jacobi Jr. Introduction by W.H. Auden.* Published in 1952 by Random House as part of something called the Modern Library and printed by the Parkway Printing Company. This would be my first meeting with Auden, in prose, as an introducer of these tales. There is no translator's name on the title page, but on the following, left-hand page, the note above the copyright bears quoting in its entirety:

> The text of the Grimm stories is based on translations by Lucy Crane, Marian Edwardes, Mrs. E.V. Lucas, Mrs. H.V. Paull, and Margaret Hunt. The text of the Andersen tales is based primarily on the Hurd and Houghton edition of *Andersen's Stories and Tales* and *Andersen's Wonder Stories* (Boston, 1871, 1872) for which no translator is listed, and partially on the translations of Mrs. E.V. Lucas and Mrs. H.V. Paull. These translations have been thoroughly revised and modernised.

On the facing page, the right-hand page, a single shapely paragraph in italics. This paragraph, the epigraph for the volume, is undersigned by "The Brothers Grimm" (not in italics). What kind of dyad would the child-reader have imagined as this doubled writer, shadow twins with a single pen? The paragraph begins with a poor boy who found a tiny gold key in the snow (the reader lives *at that time* in a place of winter snow) and ends "…and then we shall learn what wonderful things were lying in that box."

In that "box," the mise en abyme, "A Picture Book Without Pictures."
Ends: means: the mise en abyme of the story becomes the circularity,
the circulation of the song.

"with an extra gill of whiskey and a song…"
Lewis (or Clark?)

For Robert, both of them

Crayon, Issue Three
2001

(no longer or not yet…)
TRANSLATION AND THE RECOVERY
OF THE PUBLIC WORLD

"It is not the acoustics that we have to worry about: they will take
care of themselves. Rather we have to worry about distance."—Osip
Mandelstam

In this distance, which could be temporal, appear reminders that
questions of translation metaphorically or literally evoke issues of ethics,
of self and other, issues of temper and style. (Look at any considerations
of the act of translation, for instance, André du Bouchet's contemporary
"relaxing into inattention," or "The Faithful Translator" (good) vs. "The
Spirited Translator" (bad) distinctions of John Hookam Frere, 1840s,
or Philo of Alexandria's first-century "On the Confusion of Languages"
and so on.)

Distance and *desubjectivization*.

As an example of desubjectivization, Giorgio Agamben, in his
"Impropriété," which is how "Disappropriata maniera," his introduction
to Caproni's *Res amissa*, appeared in French, goes to Dante, *Purgatorio
XXIV* (lines coming directly after Dante cites himself, his "intelletto
d'amore" from the *Vita Nuova*) "I am one who," first to third person
("son un che") and then the verb is "noto," back to first person; he
could have noted Rimbaud's, "je est un autre." Or Caproni. *We* might
note Agamben's assertion that the point of contact is the still point, the
moot or mute point, and that the action, movement, can only happen
in the space between, the measure or distance; or in what Robin Blaser,
in his note appended to his Nerval translations, refers to as "between
the personal and the mysterious."

In *Infancy and History*, Agamben observes that, since Baudelaire,
poetry relies less than before, if at all, on experience, as in "the poet's
experience" or life. For him, language is a part of the birthright, what's
naturally human, like opposable thumbs or standing upright. We
have to have it. The area of overlap between the lived and the poem
is language. Distance is created in the desubjectivization the poet

experiences in writing. Consideration of the translation *of* experience as the matter of writing leads to thoughts about the pertinence of Nathaniel Mackey's reference to "modes of being prior to one's own experience," to "records of experience that are part of the communal and collective inheritance that we have access to." (interview, *Talisman 9*)

The distance is useful.

"The central model for me is troubadour poetry. Thus, my interest in foreign poetry, whether distant in time and space, linguistically or not, is only a variant, an exploration of the same type of connection, which is a relation to a past model…, distant models…." (Jacques Roubaud interview in *Toward a New Poetics: contemporary writing in France*, ed. & trans. Serge Gavronsky. University of California Press 1994)

The distance is literal and real.

Translation is always taking place in that distance, taking a measure of that distance. "Hence the vanity of translation; it were as wise to cast a violet into the crucible that you might discover the formal principle of its color and odor, as seek to transfuse…." The notation from Shelley breaks off and then my notebook says "the restfulness of the opaque areas…."

Introductory Remarks, Translation & Poetry Panel
"Recovery of the Public World," a Conference
Honoring ROBIN BLASER
Vancouver B.C.
January 1995

Published in *Recovery of the Public World:*
Essays on Poetics in Honour of Robin Blaser
eds. Ted Byrne & Charles Watts
(Talonbooks, 1999)

SINGULARITIES: THE PAINTINGS OF STANLEY WHITNEY

Color is life.... Colors are
primordial ideas....
— Alma Thomas

The first circle recapitulates the ones to come. Each one will be different. Aphoristic dashes pin them down, at first from within, later from all possible directions. The elements can't all be moving at the same time. Where hesitation becomes rhythmic assertion, a dance steps into the recognizable system of moves called the physical lyric. In its transgression of its own system, each painting questions assumptions about generalization. The universe is composed of singularities.

The painter sees with scary lucidity. His structure is a vehicle for color. The reference is color, of paint. Muscle information, seen, is *felt*, the way food, seen, is *tasted*. This is communication on a metabolic level, working you the way prosody works you, individual as a fingerprint. Each singular painting, by means of its elements, produces a dominant tone. The paintings refer to one another, participating in an ongoing conversation about color relations, drawing, placement, illusion, volume, surface, space... in their own time. And yet, they exist, sensuous *proofs* of the choices and physical movement of the one who made them.

Seeing them, you see what he's seen. Critical focus manifests itself at every point. The painting is complete attention. Its every event is new and fresh and alert. Like a musician quoting a few bars of another song in his own song, the painter, at moments, makes tonal quotes: yes, thinking of Matisse here, remembering Bob Thompson's flat emblematic use of color here, articulating the Yoruban investigation of shape's numinosity, here.

Their colors name them: the one with a frond-like shape of brilliant acidic green shadowed by the color of ripe eggplant in the upper left-hand corner of the canvas; the one with two sharp vertical assertions—black lines—in the upper left; the one with three rows of large emotional circles and only the suggestion of linear intercalation except for the vivid red line—drawn comment angled into the lower right corner of the painting. Pyramidal shapes emerge between circles, rectangles are implied or explicit: repetition's own power.

How do you begin something that has no apparent beginning? Like some poetry, like music, this painting unhooks color events from daily accountability in order to present configurations that offer experience belonging to painting, to looking at painting.

What is this persistent immediacy? The space and color of painting and the world are coextensive. Movement occurs in how the colors draw, touch and cross. The circles are made up of motion laid bare—visible the trace of brush, physical the color tracks—you see them as they are laid down, their timing, their order.

A color underneath invites another color and becomes an aside, a shadow, a memory featuring and framing color/thought/motion. Movement is contained by edges, dimensions define the territory in which compression builds. Sometimes shapes or strokes are going off the edge, or a shape is split by an edge. Containment of energy, energy of containment. Combustion takes place between and among colors, their drama in their own arena. At times, colors in proximity, in fecund intensity, perform a quiet spectacle, deliberately slow in revealing, in dazzling disclosure of marks producing time internal to painting, to the painting, its own scale.

Looking, you enter the play. The painter is working his medium, color. The painting, becoming, defines his responsibility. Color becomes its text, its object, scription, not description. Color and drawing are inseparable. Each mark knows and shows how it's made. The paintings are lush and laconic, their economy strangely like the painter's city. The painting is not a mental construct but rather something possible, becoming, specific. With mixed emotions, with openness, clarity, generosity and humor. A French poet, Edmond Jabès, once called hospitality "rainbow." Colors imagine space, time-bound.

Every day, the news is in these paintings. Each time, leaving order is a way of starting over: the painter's indomitability. *To be explicit* is a verb filled with intention, as is *to celebrate* colors' lively assertion, building.

Some of them are so open you can see right through them except that the color on top holds you from falling through and the color underneath holds up the color on top. Colors seem to know each other in ways words are not able.

In the studio the light is on. The painter is sitting in the green chair, looking, reading, looking. The fullness of space is visible.

Catalogue essay
University of Dayton
1991

Ten Minutes to Talk About Experimental Writing: A Documentary

What's the difference between the thinking word and thinking of a word, that is, between choosing a word and merely thinking the word, having the word "come up" because some association brought it to mind. An extreme of this question occurs, for instance, in the case of someone with Tourrette's Syndrome: such a person is unable to inhibit behavior that might be deemed inappropriate, rude or insulting. Seeing someone in the street, a person with TS might say aloud any epithet ever heard or overheard in relation to such a person. Words come to mind unbidden, from the fabric of the received culture, from the public realm. They are not the secret thoughts of the person with TS. He or she is not necessarily aligned emotionally or psychologically or politically with what he or she has articulated.

Such distinctions are often misunderstood in relation to writing. Even the most experienced readers who may be also writers often misunderstand or misread a complexity of presentation, identifying writer with written work as though there is a simple one-to-one correlation. That I write a word/thought/idea must mean I subscribe to it, believe it, believe in it. This misapprehension is often used to attack, on so-called political terms, the work of writers, photographers, artists of all kinds (here, of course, we think of Mapplethorpe, Kiefer, Salgado, Ian Hamilton Finlay and countless others). "no light between his him and me," a phrase from the writing of Nathaniel Mackey, seems to describe that confusion.

The verb *experiment* used to mean, according to the OED, "to have experience of; to experience; to feel, suffer," as in "Suffer the little children to come unto me," or "Whenever the mind of the artist suffers itself to be occupied during periods of its creation, by any other predominant motive than the desire of beauty, the result is false in art." (Hallam) This use of *experiment* is, according to the OED, obsolete. When I was checking these definitions after receiving a call from Andrew's assistant, Rob, asking me to prepare something to say about an issue in experimental writing for this panel, I did experience a strong and clear awareness of the arbitrariness of "my authorities." The OED is

what I choose to keep at hand, to read and plunder, to fold its lore into
what I am thinking about.

Before I began to read the definitions, or descriptions, really, of the
historical habits of use of the word *experiment*, and check its derivations
through Latin and Greek, I got a call from Steve Dickison, asking for
publisher Eck Finlay's phone number in Edinburgh. And I told him
I had just gotten the word that I was supposed to be thinking about
experiment, as in "an issue in experimental writing." And the two of us
immediately, and this was over the phone, not even able to see each
other's face, stopped as though looking at each other and shrugging,
acknowledging to each other the strangeness of that word and curious
nature of the phrase and the fact that in order to begin I'd have to "look
it up," our version of "starting from scratch" or from "what is."

The Latin *experimentum* breaks down into *experior* and *mentum*.
Experior is making a trial of, testing, putting to the test, and also
experiencing, undergoing. It has *periculum* in it, which I remembered
from my high school Latin days as having to do with danger, risk, so
there is something at stake here, which seems to refer back to experience
as suffered, undergone. *Mentum* splits into chin, and leads to idioms
that mean things like saving a life by pulling someone out of the water
presumably by their chin, and its being also the past participle of
miniscor which goes back further to the Sanskrit *manyate*, think, and
is related to the Greek *memora*, remembering, keeping in mind, being
mindful of; but, more specifically, recalling in writing, or in speech.
One particular example has it expressing or recording one's gratitude,
at which point I have made a note to remind myself that to speak is to
remember.

Earlier that day, Aaron Shurin and I had been talking about Proust
and his great work which apparently had not originally been titled *A
la recherche du temps perdu* but some other unremarkable thing that no
one remembers now unless they're reading a biography of Proust, which
Aaron is, or was then. Especially towards the end of *A la recherché...*
the narrative device is dropped and writing lets itself experience or
undergo or suffer a rapture of thought and memory in a discussion of
writing, experience and idea. Aaron was talking also about his own lack
of identification at the moment with "the poem," and about how he is

thinking more about work he has been doing that he refers to as "my AIDS essays." He has a book-length manuscript of these essays which are amazing investigations into his discovering how to think and write about that complicated and charged subject. Aaron then expressed his intention to write more "AIDS essays, but not about AIDS." So he was trying to think about what he has been working out as a form and how to use that knowledge to move into the next form. How does one move into the next form?

That afternoon I went to a tea-room in my neighborhood, a place where I sometimes go to sit and think. I was thinking about how I had been wanting to write something evoking or in relation to the independent filmmaker and critic Warren Sonbert, who had died of AIDS on May 31st. This loss, acutely felt, as well recalls other loss. I thought about Warren's films, of how their increasingly savvy and sophisticated investigation nails the viewer as the site of the constitution of "meaning." "Meaning" includes sensory and emotional as well as intellectual pleasures; and pleasure itself always implies its Other, pain, and so we are back to experience as suffering. The contradictions are inextricably tangled, indivisible.

I was thinking also of a film I'd seen with Warren just over a year ago, Ersenov's "100 Days Before the Order." During the Gay Film Festival press screening, I'd made notes and from the notes I'd written a poem and dedicated it to Warren. That is, I'd used material extracted from those notes in at least two pieces, one of which I'd dedicated to Warren, the one where the words from the title or name of the film were actually incorporated. I brought with me the notebook I had been using then, in order to look back at what I'd written that afternoon. But I always interleave ephemera into my notebooks as I use them, and so, at first I was rediscovering all kinds of things that now, a year later, were surprises. For instance, there was an excerpt from Susan Howe's "Sorting Facts; or Nineteen Ways of Looking at Marker" which begins with Dziga Vertov:

- the FACTORY OF FACTS.
  Filming facts. Sorting facts. Disseminating facts.
  Agitating with facts. Propaganda with Facts. Fists made of facts.
- Lightning flashes of facts.

- Mountains of facts.
- Hurricanes of facts.
- And individual little factlets.
- Against film-sorcery.
- Against film-mystification.
- For the genuine cinematification of the worker-peasant.

USSR 1926

Howe goes on to say, "I was asked to contribute something to this collection of essays because of a book I once wrote about Emily Dickison's poetry. Although this was a strange reason to assume I could write about non-fiction film I was drawn to the project because of the fact of my husband's death and my wish to find a way to document his life and work."

OED, *Experiment*, n. The action of trying anything, or putting it to proof; a test, a trial; a tentative procedure; a method, system of things, or course of action, adopted in uncertainty whether it will answer the purpose.

What we are doing all the time, working, thinking, feeling, studying, discussing, dreaming, groping and looking around is undergoing finding the form, its necessity.

"hold fast to yr power over old form, let you only be busted out of it like the door of a safe when some nitroglycerine you may not even yet know has been applied to the crack in yr door, blows you open"
(Charles Olson to Robin Blaser, May 1957)

"hold fast to yr power over old form...." Where I've copied this sentence into my notebook, I've added parenthetically "or old form's power over you...or, yes, the chemistry that occurs in the you/form relationship," let that reach its critical mass....

And when I mentioned this panel to Kevin Killian while we were working on a project together, he suggested I read from the notes on translation I had made for a panel at the recent events celebrating Robin Blaser in Vancouver. These notes, using "distance" as a keyword, consider, among other things, translation and experience. Here is an excerpt from them:

In *Infancy and History*, Giorgio Agamben observes that, since Baudelaire, poetry relies less than before, if at all, on experience, as in "the poet's experience" or life. For (Agamben), language is a part of the birthright, what's naturally human, like opposable thumbs or standing upright. We have to have it. The area of overlap between the lived and the poem is language. Distance is created in the desubjectivization the poet experiences in writing. Consideration of the translation of experience as the matter of writing leads to thoughts about the pertinence of Nathaniel Mackey's reference to "modes of being prior to one's own experience," to "records of experience that are part of the communal and collective inheritance that we have access to." (interview, *Talisman 9*)

Which reminds me now of that strange instance of the collision of collective and the personal that occurs in the case of the person with TS. *Experiment* is proofing something, *experimental* is relating to experience. An interesting part of the OED definition says *experimental* means based on or derived from experience as opposed to mere testimony or conjecture. What is "mere testimony and conjecture"?

But don't you find it impossible to meet continual reference to trial and test without thinking to Zukofsky's *A Test of Poetry*? Its preface begins: "The test of poetry is the range of pleasure it affords as sight, sound, and intellection. This is its purpose as art." And it ends, "I believe that desirable teaching assumes intelligence that is free to be attracted from any consideration of every day living to always another phase of existence. Poetry, as other object matter, is after all for interested people."

I will close by reading those notes called "film w/ Warren."

25.v.94

film w/ Warren

begins like someone else's memory

The contiguity of the dream

The aspect of the film that's untranslatable—What is it
being posed against & or
What norms is it superimposed on

The haze at that time of day

you don't say your thoughts

"Hold the belt" does that mean
tighten your belt or bite the
bullet?
Will there be a recurrence of
vividness? He is running lying
down they mocked you

    The morality was in the
tracking shot
Erotic, like a new idea

                            time of day, as
landscape, like
punctuation
children finding adults lying

on the ground as punctuation

repeatedly walking away or

calling as punctuation

Just as we can't know what
we're in

Excellence is translatable
               instantly

immediately. But there could be
a complexity of excellence

As if beauty were obvious

"like a bow tightly drawn"

Or by sleep
the light
even without music

The rest of them are asleep

The one who could not or would not

The image of desire to be at the

bottom of the tiled pool, in a

foetal position
Eventually the landscape the bow
tightly drawn
The table is set

We don't think about the same things
anymore or read the same books
or wait the same way

What is this luminous drawing of
triple arches on the wall, a viaduct?

AMAS

Naropa University
July 1995

Published in
Quarter After Eight
1999

IF IT WERE CHRISTA WOLF

Of all the organisms on earth, only
bacteria are individuals.
Lynn Margulis

a young poet puts himself the subjects together
Johannes Becher

I with German tongue
this cloud around me
that I keep as house
drive through all tongues
Ingeborg Bachmann

Who *writes about things that disturb her. A proposition of consciousness.*
Thought appealing to language. Feeling to thought. A composite. Little
habits of time that recur. Dream or remember the disappearance of
the photograph, an inquiring glance, tacit permission. Who *places the*
photograph in a pocket.

In Christa Wolf's writing there is a constant breaking down of subject/
object definition, both existing together within each other and without.
What's outside what outside? Endangered world, endangered persons
living in the world, can they be distinct one from the other? A person
existing within the social whole from which a person is not dividable,
separable. Writing and agency. Writing is agency. Cooking is taking
place.

By a succession or serial person *who* was an interaction between self-
determination and the interpellation of history.

An imaginary solution is not presupposed. *Who* imagines it. *Who*
misses. Agree to agree to what tools of thought. *Who* was hungry. *Who*
was looking out of those eyes. And the dog in the dream is also *who.*

Young Hellwig had been witness to all this. Ever since he had
begun to think independently, the camp had been there, and so
had the explanation for its being. He had no other knowledge.
He had still been a boy when the camp had been built. Now
he was almost a youth, and it was being built once more, so to
speak. (Anna Seghers, *The Seventh Cross*)

Someone escapes, "call him George this week," and this escape creates a
breach, a disruption. A place opens up for questions in Hellwig's mind.
Will he rebuild the camp? So to speak. *Who* gives him this choice.
Rebuilding is and is not literal, not the literal walls, which remain, but
the mechanisms of mind that retake escaped prisoners, replace them in
concentration camps.

Imagine that he comes and I signal him a warning. What will
happen to me, to us?— And then, imagine he comes and I see
him coming and I make no sign…. He is seized. Can one do
such a thing? (Anna Seghers, Ibid.)

Who asks.

What was pure instinct once
Is now done by rule.
Ovid

Sometimes we are looking at the notation of emotion.

Anna Seghers (1900-1983), mentor to Christa Wolf, was writing this
from France, in exile, having fled Germany in 1933, after Hitler became
chancellor, after the spectacle of book burning at the university in
Berlin, after her books were all placed on the Nazi blacklist, after her
apartment had been broken into by the police, after her neighbors had
hidden her…. (Her daughter writes later of how the children, with the
last of their money, were sent to swimming lessons, for, who knew, one
day perhaps they would have to continue their flight by boat.) Perhaps
in a conversation with Christa Wolf Anna Seghers says that when you

write for (30, 60, n…) years how can you separate living and writing, the lived and the written? Someone receives a book in the mail and writes back on a postcard, "It is life!"

Having eschewed product recognition for estrangement the stakes are high. "If there is an avant-garde in our time, it is probably bent on discovery through suicide." (Ihab Hassan, *The Postmodern Turn*) The writing of this Christa Wolf would not fall into such a category of avant-garde.

Memory outlasts the series of subjects, connects them. Sooner or later there is imitation and relief. *Whose* hands exceed the frame. The permeability of narration, increasing permeability of "characters" in the "story" which is "true." The assumptions of permanence about a name, its continuity, for example, are continuously thrown into question.

> Corrections: A man in the news article yesterday about Egon Krenz, the new East German leader, referred incorrectly to his native town, Kohlberg. It is now called Kolobrzeg and has been a part of Poland since 1945. (*New York Times*, 10.20.89)

Reason is also proposed as a function of memory, "a repeated moral act." (CW *The Quest for Christa T*)

"But the third person stands by and records what the second does to the first." (Ibid.) People are formed in their memories of each other as they mirror each other. Different sets of eyes and desires form the outcome.

September 26, 1989. Nancy Spero: "And so we think about war and total destruction." *Who* sees what *who* never thought existed. Do more names permit more birds? Do all the stories cluster around entity/memory/idea(l)?

A merging with the predicate and sometimes a separation. A threading and fraying took place. Take place. It is not about empathy, although empathic response is not precluded. No one is larger. The persons, layered, shattered, exposed, are flawed.
"Human." Their impulses conflict, contradict. There is a presentation of a "reality," a "truth" emerging from dream and imagination, emotion

and event. Characters are propositions of a new knowledge which constructs feelings and imaginings as characters. Memory is one thing, evidence another.

"Natural" is continuously questioned. For instance, "common sense" as natural, "feelings" as natural, unmediated by culture, ideology. People who occupy social positions, as we all do, occupy their roles. Social understandings require certain labels
for certain responses to given events. For instance, in some cultures people are trained to associate pleasure with the acquisition of goods, with shopping. *Who* asks why.

> Of course there was more glass and more glitter in the shop windows in West Berlin, and there were things to buy which she had never even seen before. But she had known that already. She had liked all that, too, and had thought it would be fun to go shopping there. Still, all those things were connected to eating and drinking, clothes and sleeping. But why did one eat? (CW *Divided Heaven*)

Who is asking why.

To keep separate and direct or to reconfigure and act. "The need to write in a new way follows a new way of living in the world, although there may be a time lag." (CW *Reader and Writer*) *Context*, what was once called fate? *Action*, the collision of thought and language into writing?

Style as proposed by Barthes in *Writing Degree Zero* is the intersection of time and biology. Writing is proposed as the connector between creation and the social, or as Christa Wolf might say, between creation and the social.

> (the biologists) informed us that we should first of all not be amazed at the changing nature but at the continuity of biological forms, the complicated mechanism that enables the genes to reproduce themselves repeatedly, a mechanism unknown until recently. (CW *Reader and Writer*)

Known, unknown, it functions. If only there were roadside bookstores everywhere and buses to take us there.

Readiness is a state experienced by *whom*, which allows certain things to happen. Readiness is not the same thing as prescience, nor does it assume a template for all future action and/or circumstance. Readiness is fluidity precluding separation from event. It is not a dialectical notion. Contradictions occur. Parts =/= whole. People, being countries, have territory. And if the borders are eliminated. And is the state of thought independent of the thinker.

> Kleist has never before been among people who trespass so greatly on each other's territory and yet do not become enemies as a result.... He stretched out and experienced in body and limbs what freedom is, without a word even once entering his mind. (CW *No Place On Earth*)

	means		
before	SELF	SELF	(Descartes etc.)
	makes		

	means		
after	OTHER	SELF	(Deleuze etc.)
	makes		

"We used to be truly thankful whenever we were able to picture an idea." (CW *Accident*) "I was this" (Clark Coolidge) In this case, I permitted myself, my position, i.e. my experience, to tell me; and the language, in this case reprimand, proceeded from it.
Givens are no mother for circumstances. *just a thing being done to people in the name of a system* Anguish and orders going from action itself to some future writing is between. "Where we've all been for a while"—name, thought can join to form epithet. Future memory can be constructed action now. Christa Wolf impairs narrative.

> *With my burned hand*
> *I write about the nature of fire*
> Ingeborg Bachmann

"whose sentence it measures out"
Michael Palmer

Capriciousness has no place here. *Who* wills *whose* will.

Nelly, the little girl of *A Model Childhood* (also known as *Patterns of Childhood*), is constructed to embody, to impersonate the child Christa Wolf might remember was herself. The narrator describes the child's feeling that to have taken a prescribed position on things, everything, would have been more comfortable for her. She was not "one" with all the "correct responses." *Whose* welling up of tears was an inappropriate response, punishable. Such memories are "engraved" by "guilt." *Who* could feel "only that which has been decreed?" In Nelly's schoolgirl life the only greeting permitted was "Heil Hitler." Another "hello" did not exist. "A person who wants to pass unnoticed soon stops noticing anything." *Who* disappeared—into—action?

They were deeply engrossed in something, by something, a fire, a baby…. Interrupted, they were embarrassed and had to suppress emotions they had not yet named. Anxious, dreaming mediations, internalized, proceed to construct. This writing is lifting scabs a reader/writer might have forgotten or wanted to forget exist. Poetics of investigation, never reassuring, never relying on the pleasure of recognition, familiarity. "The moon had risen, but outside your field of vision." (CW *A Model Childhood*) This is social space in distress, troubled, vision doubled, every place taken over, changed, erased, named and renamed.

> You closed your eyes and saw a clear and accurate image of the market square in L. (formerly G.) as Nelly had known it, and you found it difficult to visualize it in its present state, as you had just seen it. (Ibid.)

If… then….

If Person is formed and informed by *time* (memory, interpellation, will) and *function* (conditions or a series of moments intersecting with the individual set) then what happens in a "vacuum," i.e., sudden elimination of "conditions"?

Christa Wolf, the novelist, was one of the leading speakers at a rally of one million East Berliners.... Last week she completed the final draft of an appeal entitled "For Our Country," which argues for protecting the separate identity of the German Democratic Republic from West German encroachment. The appeal has already been signed by a quarter of a million citizens. (*New York Times* 12.9.89)

Birds are flying south in formation. Occupation is the ongoing condition of occupying or being occupied. What determines one's inner resources at a time like this, i.e., at any time?

In 1918, in *Geist der Utopie*, Ernst Bloch wrote, "I am. We are. That is enough. Now it is up to us to begin." In 1945, Sartre wrote, in *L'Existentialisme est un humanisme*, which was presented as a lecture, "Man is nothing other than what he does."

"I wonder if I should buy my son's new shoes now or wait until the revolution." (Cab driver from Yugoslavia, *New York Times* 11.25.89) Proceed with the telling.

> *in the telling*
> *I happens*
> Michael Davidson

"Could she bear the sudden liberation from the old ideas of what was possible?" (CW *Divided Heaven*) "I saw a news item turn into truth." (CW *Cassandra*)

Selected Bibliography

Bachmann, Ingeborg, "Exil." In *German Poetry 1910-1975*, first authorized American edition, edited by Michael Hamburger. (my trans.)

Barthes, Roland, *Le Degré zéro de l'écriture*. Paris 1953

Becher, Johannes, "Die Neue Syntax." In *German Poetry 1910-1975* as cited above. (my trans.)

Bloch, Ernst, *The Utopian Function of Art and Literature: Essays*. MIT 1988

Davidson, Michael, "Hypothesis." *Hambone 8*

Hassan, Ihab, *The Postmodern Turn*. Ohio 1987

Lutz, Catherine A., *Unnatural Emotions*. Chicago 1988

Margulis, Lynn, from some magazine in some dentist's office, 1989

Ovid, "Cures for Love." In *Erotic Poems*. UK 1987

Palmer, Michael, "Baudelaire Series." *Sun*. San Francisco 1988

Sartre, Jean-Paul, *L'Existentialisme est un humanisme*. Paris 1967

Seghers, Anna, *The Seventh Cross*. New York 1987

Wolf, Christa, *Accident*. New York 1989
_____, *A Model Childhood*. New York 1980
_____, *Cassandra*. New York 1984
_____, *Divided Heaven*. GDR 1965
_____, *No Place On Earth*. New York 1982
_____, *Reader and Writer*. GDR 1977
_____, *The Quest For Christa T.* New York 1970

Other Sources

Hutcheon, Linda, *The Politics of Postmodernism*. UK 1989

Smith, Paul, *Discerning the Subject*. Minnesota 1988

Therborn, Goran, *The Ideology of Power and the Power of Ideology*. UK 1980

Wolf, Christa, *The Fourth Dimension: Interviews With Christa Wolf.* UK 1988

Worpole, Ken, *Dockers and Detectives.* UK 1983

Sulfur 34
Spring 1994

Yellow and...

But this began with a question about yellow. Cadmium Yellow Light and Cadmium Yellow Lemon, what does it mean that they are both called yellow? In her Artist's Statement (undated) Welish speaks about her use of diptych "to announce that this physical difference will be realized also as formal difference." She writes, "Current projects also include paintings whose structure of difference presents two competing yellows, two competing reds and two competing blues, to ask the question: which is the 'true' one (the relative rather than the absolute condition of norms is thereby revealed)."

About yellow, Goethe wrote in his *Theory of Colours*, "This is the colour nearest the light." And "In its highest purity it always carries with it the nature of brightness, and it has a serene, gay, softly exciting character." "Hence in painting it belongs to the illumined and emphatic side."

Color is a pan-species perception. Color discrimination is an activity in the brain. That is, in humans, it is dependent upon an underlying neural structure, a neural basis of sensation. It is not a cultural construction and does not depend on language. It is not solely a function of the wavelengths of light. It is not just a function of the atomic structure of the object. It is not simply generated by light upon the object of perception. We humans have color constancy, which is to say we recognize a color as "the same" regardless of whether its wavelength is entirely changed by being seen in red sunlight or blue fluorescent light. Our experience of color is physical, cognitive, not a function of consciousness or of naming. Prior to the work of neuroscientists such as Maturana & Varela, Varela, Thompson and Rosch, color theorist and psychologist Faber Birren might have found this kin to, or a form of, eidetic imagery.

In the beginning I wanted to talk about the painting. However, without having seen, actually physically having seen, the paintings, I could not speak (write) about them.

One way to address both the painting impulse and the poetry impulse was to consider how Welish has written about painting and use that writing as the journal work, the commonplace book, as her "other" for poetry. This would be an accommodation to both, as well as a speculation about sets of relationships or possible relationships.

In the beginning I thought I could talk about the painting and the poetry together, how they both find their origins in "a smudge, a dot, a line," the "not very noble" "unpromising" initial and initiating expressions, "physically slight though they may be."

All of this under the rubric of "yellow and..." our investigation of its absolute, relational, formal, compositional, eidetic and physical, neural qualities. Aural values, rhythmic values, translations?

The focus on *competition* in the repeated phrase "two competing yellows," and so on, began to attract attention to itself. After all, Welish could have expressed these relationships in more general terms of comparison, acts of bringing together, com. "Comparison" is from *compare,* to speak of or represent as similar, to liken, making parallelisms that don't quite match up; and Welish was interested in difference. "Competition" is from *competere,* to fall together, coincide, come together. *Petere* itself is to fall upon, assail, aim at, make for, try to reach, strive after, sue for, solicit, ask or seek. In its post-classical sense it is to enter into or be put into rivalry with, to vie with another in any respect. (OED)

Can't have difference without the other thing. The repetition. Rhythm of repetition. Redundancy, even. Difference in repetition. It becomes interesting to frame or undermine these considerations of competitive relationality with a reading of the use of *simile* in Welish's poetry. Think of it: diptych and simile. There is something of the deep structure of comparison to be addressed here. And by "deep structure" I refer to work currently being done by linguists who are tracking simile not as the trivial poetic figure Williams scorned, a rhetorical gesture, a figure of speech—but as a fundamental neural, cognitive, epistemological tool.

A structure of *finding out.* (We'll leave the metaphorical possibilities of "finding out" to George Lakoff and move on.) So we have the structure of comparison active as a questioning as well as compositional "idea of form" in the paintings, and we have the structure of comparison using the parallelism of simile as a means of composition in the poetry,

through comparison, through composed. Simile in the most open
sense: explicit or implicit parallel structure of *like* or *as*, often extended,
unpleating image in rhythmizing measure, for instance from *Casting
Sequences*, title poem, 4)

of actuality.
    Of actual number, pale
and spelled in cold,

a contiguity defying visual markers of line, period, space, reiteration
with difference, accumulating force in surprising acts of accretion and
elimination. Do the terms compete?

The theory of tragedy, in this view, does not separate
actor and spectator but extends indefinitely to the farmer
walking behind his plough…
(*CS* 26,2)

"Logic through lyric is, arguably, intriguing" ("The Logics," *else, in
substance*)

Yellow and…

Yellow pigments:
Ochre, transparent
gold ochre, raw
sienna, Mars yellow,
the cadmiums

    From pale primrose to
deep
  orange, a
wide   assortment
of shades. Permanent for all
techniques but
fresco

Identical to cadmium
reds insofar as

pigment properties and
permanence are concerned

Naples yellow, strontium
yellow, cobalt yellow, hansa
yellow, Nickel-azo yellow.

Inferior and obsolete
yellow pigments: chrome
yellows and oranges, Indian
yellow, yellow lakes, Dutch pink
stil-de-grain, not
permanent.
Yellow's changing
music changes.

But we are not looking at the yellows just now but at the syntax, the
inner structure of comparison as a means of making order, changing
order, ideas of order. The syntax of diptych like or as simile.

Initial point of order: repetition. Repetition as enchantment,
incantation, extension, elaboration, registration: the beguiling text that
lives within the title, *Begetting Textile*. The *beguine's* practice accords
the viewer, reader, listener, farmer, dance partner a greater role in the
completion, or lack of completion of, the accomplishment of, the work.
Perhaps completion bears no mention here. The *béguine,* however, was
a member of a lay sisterhood in the Netherlands in the 13th century
before she became the name of a ballroom dance, based on a rumba-
like dance from Martinique named after the *béguin*, the hood worn in
the sisterhood, begetting *beguine*, text of flirtation. And in 1935, Cole
Porter's "Begin the Beguine," from the musical, "Jubilee." Moments
divine, rapture serene, begin the beguine.
"As a tourist aches, as a tourist experiences the entailment
of Europe without words and only a wallet to express,
feeling adult but stored within the body of an infant,"
("A Way of Life," *The Windows Flew Open*)

"O mathematicians, shed light on
error such as this! The spirit has no

voice, because where there is voice
there is body."
Leonardo da Vinci

Although where there is body there is not always yet voice.

Repetition, its pre-echo. In the beginning is rhythm. This is the point of departure as well as the *point de repère*, point of reference, guide. This is repetition and difference. The diptych.

"...recurrent architectural strategies: one sees irony and enchantment, an evocative rather than archeological use of antiquity, a bricolage of references, the use of off-balance and ingenuous perspective, a predilection for secluded spaces that seem suspended from gravity." (Fulvio Irace, "Precursors of Modernism: Milan 1920-1930")

     ...In this going abroad
(*CS42*)

the solid observer antecedes the rebirth
of space. Yet, another voice breaks,
then successively

new excrescences of the invisible
aural spectacle move a process
well in advance of seeing.

Singing perhaps, in polyrhythmic color, in cubist progressions, even achromatic, rhythms visible as wave patterns used in Polynesian navigation where there are long distances to travel over open seas with no fixed locating points.

When is a metaphysical plaster like a matrix? How does paralysis suddenly function like a prompt? By wishing, as in

Wishing to make a metaphysical plaster
Wishing to be a matrix
(both capitalized Ws)

...

...paralysis prompts our plan

of non-identical yet necessarily correlated colonnades—
(*CS* 37)

Multiple pulse. Repetition in DNA leads to new organs with new
functions. Repetition, the simplest form of redundancy (a term
having suddenly acquired renewed currency through its use value for
information theory), leads, in time, to chance mutations, the redundant
genes ceasing to be copies and becoming unique sequences. The timing
of expression of a gene that was part of a regulatory system would
alter, altering function, contributing entirely new meaning. (Campbell,
Grammatical Man)
At first it looked like repetition, but later it became apparent that
the rhythm involved beginning and beginning again, a recuperation
through the implied—or implicate?—series of beginning—again.

Differing from Freudian interpretation, speculation by Benjamin
(Mehlman, *Benjamin's Radio for Children*) and others has it that
repetition is a means of dealing with trauma. Perhaps you recall a
passage from Deleuze and Guattari's *A Thousand Plateaus* (311, in
"1837: Of the Refrain") which begins:
"A child in the dark, gripped with fear, comforts himself by singing
under his breath."
And the paragraph finishes,
"But the song itself is already a skip: it jumps from chaos to the
beginning of order in chaos and is in danger of breaking apart at any
moment. There is always sonority in Ariadne's thread. Or the song of
Orpheus."

The thread and the song.
"Marching orders, it's murdering my sense of rhythm and making me
crazy." (Khlebnikov, *The King of Time*) One's own rhythmizing impulse
makes song, repetition expresses new function, whereas imposed
metrics are crazy-making and life-threatening. There is an unforeseeable
homeostatic relationship between rhythm and expectation, "a constantly
renewable expectation in movement, never a sense of satiety," writes
Kolakowsky. ("The Myth of Love," in *The Presence of Myth*)

"Logic through lyric is, arguably, intriguing,
and a lure for more of it.
The logic of love is fascination..."
(from "The Logics," fifth of the seven poems in *else, as substance*)

Expectations need repetition with disturbance. Like genetic forms, art forms change, as Shklovsky wrote, "in order to preserve the perceptibility of life." (*Mayakovsky and His Circle* 67) The ideas of order change in the progressions. As ideas of order shift new logics are revealed "in the event." This logic is *rhythmic* event. After all, if the mind as Spinoza would have it is just an idea of the body then thought—why not?—is rhythm's accomplishment. Proceeding in cascades on the order of parallel distribution or simultaneity, ideas of order are physical. And this is where the painting and the poem are not separate. Poem as symposium, art as forum?

"...a constantly renewable expectation in movement, never a sense of satiety." A wholeness without completion. A potential wholeness, a phantom limb. Energy's charge accretes in the gaps.
"As if," "as if," "as if..." (*BT*)

"But our minds at some point...began to consider the way they themselves work." (Naomi Goldblum, *The Brain-Shaped Mind*) The poem is a mind-reader, beginning at some point to consider how it works. Implicate type without token. Token is the individual reading. Your firing neurons. Cascading neurotransmitter. Your receptors. Cascades of activation. Thus yellow and...parallel distribution, interleaving disturbances of a certain order. In a certain order of form.

The poem is a mind-reader, "mapping neuronal configurations onto thoughts...to read other people's minds as well" (Goldblum) is not exactly what she says, but by simply eliminating a few words, some code, I make her say this, map a different thought. I'm reading her reading, her neuronal and semantic mapping of a thought and its rhythm and its thought begins to move.

As if
            answerable to anthem
                                        in antis

Even as

Insofar as

as
            as illustrated
                        As illustrated milk
spilt on printers' ink, throughout the protest movement
                                                            sparkling
rhetoric!
("Textile 2," *BT*)

A kind of sonic orchestration takes place, out of the waves, making
durable form in the registration itself. The registration is in terms
of conventions, agreeing and/or breaking with conventions. Like
innovation and improv in jazz, the degree of distance from conventions,
from use, plays upon the expectations (nerves) of the reader/listener.
This is where the issue of perceptibility comes in. The metaphor of
the horizon proves useful here: horizon of perceptibility. Threshold of
registration. As the poem says, "close as likeness."

"Rhythmico-syntactical figures had been predetermining the thought
process."
(Shklovsky, *Mayakovsky and his Circle*)

"I walk, swinging my arms, and mumbling still almost wordlessly; now,
I slow down so as not to interrupt my mumbling; now I mumble more
rapidly to keep in time with my steps.
"So the rhythm is trimmed and shaped, for it is the basis of all poetry
and runs through it like a roar. Gradually, out of this roar, one starts to
pick out separate words." (Mayakovsky, *How Are Verses Made?*)

Aggregate as idea of order. And speaking of syntax, there is the rhythmic
structure of simile as in "Personal letters are like a greenhouse, the
chiasm of touch." There is the likeness, in a context or matrix of

potential difference. All the possible differences cluster about the binary: if the hill were *really* like the issues, increasing as distance decreases.... A drawing near becomes a translation. Picture near rhyme and off-rhyme, their rhetoric framing and containing difference, catching difference in order to study its motives, if it had motives. Its idea of order. Apposite. Unreasonable.

"I had left my house to relax from some tedious piece of work by walking and by a consequent change of scene." (Paul Valéry, "Poetry and Abstract Thought") A shake-up is necessary. Mayakovsky said, "take a bus." The jolting is appalling. A rhythmic figure regenerates—itself again but changed because changed in the repetition, thickened or quickened.

"As I went along the street where I live, I was suddenly *gripped* by a rhythm which took possession of me and soon gave me the impression of some force outside of myself. It was as though someone else were making use of my *living-machine*. Then another rhythm overtook and combined with the first, and certain strange *transverse* relations were set up between these two principles (I am explaining myself as best I can). They combined the movement of my walking legs and some kind of song I was murmuring, or rather which was being murmured *through me*. This composition became more and more complicated and soon in its complexity went far beyond anything I could reasonably produce with my ordinary, usable rhythmic faculties."

He goes on to talk about music, dream, error and gift. And then it was over. The unexpected had happened and was gone. It left this other order as its evidence....

How to organize (shape, compose) time, in time. Repetition is binding. Spell-binding inexhaustible fundamental: an engineering "we must enter shyly, as in 'I have no idea.'" ("Preparing a Length of Arc," *The Annotated "Here"*)

"A rhythm which cuts and defines another rhythm must leave room for the other rhythm to be heard clearly." (John Miller Chernoff, *African Rhythm and African Sensibility: Aesthetics and Social Action in African Musical Idioms*)

"It is as essentially other that the other must be seen." (Jean Pouillon, *Fétiches sans fétichisme*)

"…wanting to come to a common language, one cleared of personality, having its meanings in the community of meanings." (Robert Duncan, unpublished letter to Denise Levertov, July 22, 1966)

The rhythmic level is available unfetishized otherness held in common. "To beguile many and be beguiled by one." (*CS* 13)

Visual rhythms register repetition and difference, expectation and surprise, for instance, in the violent disjunction of "fire*light*" (*CS* 56) a struggle within the word. Will it fly apart? Time will tell.

The tragic clock becomes the comic clock where "Suppressed Misfortunes" (*CS* 57) plays out insistence in hilarious fake palindromes, serial reversals, rehearsals in which a finitude is revealed to be contained by the space of history, by the time of comic gesture, Brechtian in its strange-making frontality. Repetition of form allows a tension to develop as coordinates pull apart, false subjects to false predicates overexposing syntax, its traces fading out in rhythmic echo called "music" and "memory."

"All Nature is but Art, unknown to thee…" (Pope quoted in Mehlman).
Wallace Stevens, in his lecture, "The Relations Between Poetry and Painting," quotes a revealing passage from Leo Stein's *Appreciations*. In Stein's chapter "On Reading Poetry and Seeing Pictures," he describes how, as a child, "he became aware of composition in nature and gradually realized that art and composition are one. He began to experiment as follows:

> I put on the table…an earthenware plate…and this I looked at every day for minutes or for hours. I had in mind to see it as a picture, and waited for it to become one. In time it did. The change came suddenly."

Everything, including the design on the plate, became part of the larger composition, which indicated to Leo Stein that he was beginning to see pictorially, rhythmically.

Subsequently, Stevens places "a jar in Tennessee,/And round it was, upon a hill."

This act of composition, which "made the slovenly wilderness/Surround that hill" is the one explored further, much further, by Welish's "Thing Receiving Road," an "aggregate" of five poems which, in the journal *New American Writing* No.17, includes a "Supplement" not included in *The Annotated "Here" and Selected Poems.* What's in question is the "so-called natural state," Stevens's provocative "cultural infiltration" of this "so-called natural state of perception with a first line that does not find things in nature so much as *place* them as nature." Her poems are "ruminations on the fiction established through such a maneuver."

As nature, in nature. The nature of the poems, Welish's poems, is to make an address beginning with "Still Life," in a stillness that is gathering. It is gathering its address, an energy, as it begins to speak "Of address, or else/ slow to be// secreted in Tennessee..." As the lines lengthen and the rhythmic impulses quicken and complicate, overtaking one another, knotting and releasing, the story of the "choice by Wallace Stevens to render the natural world cultural through artifice" plays out. Ruminations are extensions and also exist in their own right, having no need of "Supplement." They repeat and change the work of composition described by Stevens and before him by Stein in a radical movement of macrorhythms.

Yellow and...
involves a whole of composition that includes fragment, gap, rupture and suture.

Yellow and...
could simply point to the glasses of mango and papaya *jugos* on a table in a restaurant in Minneapolis.

Selected Bibliography

Abraham, Nicholas. *Rhythms: On the Work, Translation, and Psychoanalysis*. Collected and presented by Nicholas T. Rand and Maria Torok. Trans. Benjamin Thigpen and Nicholas T. Rand. California: Stanford University Press 1995

Berger, John. *Permanent Red*. NY & UK: Writer and Readers Publishing Cooperative Ltd. 1979

Birren, Faber. *Color Psychology and Color Therapy*. NJ: The Citadel Press 1961

Campbell, Jeremy. *Grammatical Man: Information, Entropy, Language and Life*. NY: Simon and Schuster 1982

Chernoff, John Miller. *African Rhythm and African Sensibility: Aesthetics and Social Action in African Musical Idioms*. IL: University of Chicago Press 1979

Damasio, Antonio. *The Feeling of What Happens: Body, and Emotion in the Making of Consciousness*. San Diego, NY, London: Harcourt, Inc. 1999

Deleuze, Gilles and Felix Guattari. *A Thousand Plateaus: Capitalism & Schizophrenia*. Trans. and Foreword by Brian Massumi. MN: University of Minnesota Press 1987

Goldblum, Naomi. *The Brain-Shaped Mind: What the Brain Can Tell Us About the Mind*. UK: 2001

Goethe, Johann Wolfgang Von. *Theory of Colours*. Trans. Charles Lock Eastlake. MA: MIT Press 1970

Gregory, R.L. *Eye and Brain: the psychology of seeing*. NY & Toronto: McGraw Hill 1977

Irace, "Precursors of Modernism: Milan 1920-1930," *The Skin and the Bone: From the Files of Milanese Architecture 1920-1930s*. NY: Architectural League 1982

Khlebnikov, Velimir. *The King of Time*. Trans. Paul Schmidt. NY: Dia Art Foundation 1985

Kolakowski, Leszek. *The Presence of MYTH*. Trans. Adam Czerniawski.

Chicago & London: University of Chicago Press 1989

LeDoux, Joseph. *Synaptic Self: How Our Brains Become Who We Are.* NY: Viking 2002

Maturana, Humberto and Francisco Varela. *The Tree of Knowledge: The Biological Roots of Human Understanding.* Trans. Robert Paolucci. Boston & London: Shambhala 1992

Mayakovsky, Vladimir. *How Are Verses Made?* Trans. G.M. Hyde. UK: Cape Editions 1970

Mehlman, Jeffrey. *Walter Benjamin for Children: An Essay on his Radio Years.* Chicago & London: University of Chicago Press 1993

Shklovsky, Viktor. *Mayakovsky and his Circle.* Trans. Lily Feiler. NY: Dodd & Mead 1972

Stevens, Wallace. "The Relations Between Poetry and Painting," *Collected Poetry and Prose.* NY: Library of America 1997

Valéry, Paul. "Poetry and Abstract Thought," *The Art of Poetry.* Trans. Denise Folliot. NY: Vintage 1961

Varela, Francisco J., Evan Thompson and Eleanor Rosch. *The Embodied Mind: Cognitive Science and Human Experience.* MA: MIT Press 1991

Welish, Marjorie. Published and unpublished works, letters, conversations.

"Introducing Marjorie Welish"
Slought Foundation at University of Pennsylvania
5 April 2002

Published in
Of the Diagram: The Work of Marjorie Welish
(Slought Books, 2003)

Why I Am Not A Translator—Take 2

I was going to talk about why I am not a translator but I'm not. I do translations, I've done many, mostly from French to English, but I still don't think of myself as a translator.

I had given a talk on translation at Suzanne Stein's sublet in San Francisco a year and a half ago, to friends that had gathered around her dining table, a talk titled "Why I Am Not A Translator" that began with a list of subordinate clauses I handed out, starting with "what," as in "What Rosmarie Waldrop has to do with it," "What Claude Royet-Journoud has to do with it," "What Stacy Doris has to do with it," "What Etel Adnan & Simone Fattal have to do with it," etc. Every one of them had gotten me to translate any number of books, but it was always so much more than what one thinks of as translating. Sure, it was pretty much straight-ahead translation—if you can say "straight-ahead" for the kind of experimental poetry I work on, but it was more exciting, more irritating, more crooked. More about editing than you'd think. But mostly I thought—and think—about it in terms of poetics.

At the same time as I was thinking about translation, about AWP, and about this 10-minute talk I am actually starting to give right now, I was reading René Daumal's *Rasa or Knowledge of the Self*, particularly an essay called "To Approach the Hindu Poetic Art." As some of you know, René Daumal was a French writer born in 1908 in Charleville, the same town where Arthur Rimbaud had been born in 1854. Daumal, a writer of the *avant-garde*, who penned, among his many essays, poems and novels, the acclaimed unfinished novel *Mount Analogue*, at sixteen taught himself Sanskrit, wrote a Sanskrit grammar and translated some very important texts including the *Chandyoga Upanishad* and the *Bhagavad Gita*. With failing health, hiding out in Paris during the Occupation with his wife, who was part Jewish, he died of tuberculosis in May 1944, just two weeks before the Allies landed in France.

I was reading Daumal's essay and thinking about my class at the University of San Francisco, and about the course in "Visionary Poetics" I'm teaching, and about the things I wanted to make sure to discuss with my students, and I ran across these sentences:

"The existence of thought without words but not without forms is nevertheless necessary, for example, to all translation work. Every good translator does his utmost, without actually realizing it, to translate his text first into *sphota*, in order to translate into the second language; but he would be an even better translator if he were consciously aware of this process."

I'd obviously run across these sentences many a time before, but suddenly I started to think about them in a more concentrated way.

First, the word *sphota*, what does it mean? We have to go back a paragraph: "Is there, between words and things, a rapport of simple convention or an eternal appropriateness?" In other words, the rapport of simple convention means the normal words syntax depends upon, like prepositions, or "sonorous words" (*dhvani*), the onomatopoeic and alliterative, as in
Hark! Hark!
The dogs do bark!
whereas the eternal appropriateness means ideas that preexist words and objects. Word-seeds. *Sphota*.

Ideas that preexist words and objects. A test case in neurobiology: when I had my stroke 4 years ago, two areas of language were affected. One was a motor problem. Speech production was knocked out in the brain. Therefore I couldn't talk at all. And I've had to refigure, little by little, how to make speech occur with mouth, teeth, tongue. Think of Christopher Reeves in the swimming pool, trying to make his legs function. And then, for many people who've had strokes, the brain swells, doesn't settle for a while (perhaps two or three months), so we have aphasia and can't think of words: the words for up or down, the simply conventional words; and the words that stand for ideas. I am here to tell you that one has ideas even before one has the words to say them. Ideas, or images. No *tabula rasa*.

So, that being the case, "every good translator does his utmost, without actually realizing it, to translate his text first into *sphota*, in order to retranslate it into the second language...."

I am not altogether happy with this. I mean, why shouldn't one pass from the word in the first language straight to the word in the second language, without even thinking about ideas?

"I'll reveal for you, in words as simple as mooing," says Mayakovsky.

> *"I would like*
> > *to live*
> > > *and die in Paris"*

he wrote, translated by Stephen Rudy.

> *"I would like*
> > *to live*
> > > *and die in Paris*
> *if there weren't*
> > *such a land*
> > > *as Moscow"*

and you can't change that line, Mayakovsky said. It would not be the same if you were to write "Berlin" and "Warsaw," for instance.

Or Dixie. To live and die in Dixie.

Roman Jakobson, the genius of structural linguistics, among whose great works are *Verbal Art, Verbal Sign, Verbal Time*, has written, "...the speaker selects words and combines them into sentences according to the syntactic system of the language he is using; sentences in their turn are combined into utterances. But the speaker is by no means a completely free agent in his choice of words: his selection (except for the rare case of actual neology) must be made from the lexical storehouse which he and his addressee possess in common." This is from his essay, "Two Aspects of Language and Two Types of Aphasic Disturbances," *Language in Literature*, p.97.

Paris and Moscow, Berlin and Warsaw, both dyads would be available from the lexical storehouse, but, as we know, one expresses Mayakovsky's idea, the other does not. "The 'body' of the poem is created from 'sounds and meanings,'" (Jakobson) whether it is a translation or not. But it's all translation anyhow. Crooked translation.

Panel on Translation
AWP Atlanta
March 2007

Published in
Denver Quarterly
Volume 41, Number 4, 2007

AT ALL
(Tom Raworth and His Collages)

We can at least draw courage from Schiller's letters. He sketches man as
being subject to two opposing forces. The urge of the senses insists on
change, while that towards form decrees laws. The conflict between the
two would continue together forever were it not for a third urge to act
as mediator. Thus it is the aesthetic dimension that restores unity and it
does so in the urge to play. Play is, after all, free as air, but at the same
time it cannot do without rules. The game is an order. The aesthetic
form is of the highest order.
           Alexander van Grevenstein, "*DE AEDIBUS SACRIS* AND ON BEAUTY"
                        SOL LEWITT WALL DRAWINGS 1968-1984

What if, in the non-oppositional mode, he drew upon the senses to
begin to make this form, and made play of the laws?

fluidity from
thing (picture of)
          (object)
to
  word
thing to thing
word to word

glove, face, tourniquet
landscapes
seen from the air
Gauguin's sleeper's face
rose, and rose, and lily
         of the Val
(I want to turn them
upside down)

"'Things' are transformed into 'presences.'"
           David Robbins, *The Independent Group: Post-War Britain
                    and the Aesthetics of Plenty.* MIT 1990

new circulation patterns
"HE MOVES UP"
Matisse and a piece of
cake
or what looks like
a piece of cake

rhyming twins
word to word
word to thing
thing to thing
       involves syntax

(?monochromatic at first)
shades of gray/brown/yellow
method & technique
i.e. restricted palette
shimmers
chromatism based on
equalized color
contrast equalization
of intensities

stage, staging?
Have you left something out:
"Negative, says my Gunslinger,
no thing is omitted."

Edward Dorn, *Gunslinger*
Wingbow Press, 1975

a way of working, a way
of being, maybe a kind of
rest. Tension→ease→tension
→ease. Silence in the space
around. Like comics, "the
comics," "funny papers." A

kind of serious play. A serious
playful resting place.

"And the inestimable
surveillance begins to drip
and drip."

Jess, *Tricky Cad Case V*

shards squared off
at first glance chaos
in a box melts away
seemingly seamless
and then the seams
come in to play
            motion and rest

"a crossword puzzle burning
in the originalll"

Ibid.

black cloud or a tree
meadow, meadow, lion
lion
ground comes to the fore

(He could have cut and pasted them, then cut them up into squares,
arranged them and pasted them down, we don't know.)

because each little square
is its own vertiginous
place
to create a disturbance

quietly

the white space between
is pristine, it goes on
for ever—and yet
at the same time one
sees
a checkerboard of
resistance, places
distinct all the same
is the logic of
its design

many edges to climb
over

now even
red wing
he moves

"*Fait* (Fact) is as much a physical experience as an intellectual and
emotional one. Enveloped by the shifting stances, confused by
the absence of recognizable scale and loss of perspective in these
intentionally abstract details, the viewer is left to his own conclusions,
and even with a sense of vertigo."
                    Sophie Ristelheuber: Details of the World
                 text Cheryl Brutvan. MFA Publications, 2001

"The eye cannot fix itself to any path or cloud. There is no escape."
                    Quote from Sophie Ristelheuber

the analogical mode of
thought, a picture
window, the *dominant*
(the 5th degree of major or

minor scale, or the harmony
based around that note
or a gene, its
characteristic)
torn from the same page

April 22 1663, Leeches in Vinegar. Bluish Mold on Leather; April 29th,
A Mine of Diamonds in Flint. Spider with Six Eyes; May 6th, Female
and Male Gnats; May 20th, Head of Ant. Fly like a Gnat. Point of
a Needle; May 27th, Pores in Petrified Wood. Male Gnat; June 10th,
Sage-Leaves appearing not to have cavities; July 8th, Edge of a Razor.
Five Taffeta Ribbons. Millepede; July 16th, Fine Lawn. Gilt Edge of
Venice Paper; August 5th, Honeycomb Sea-weed. Teeth of a Snail. Plant
growing on Rose-Leaves.
    From Robert Hooke's journal, *Micrographia; or, Some Physiological
    Descriptions of Minute Bodies Made by Magnifying Glasses,
    with Observations and Inquiries There Upon* (1665)

July 19 2005, Photo squares (from Tom's Birthday Walk, www.
tomraworth.com/notes/) 4 X 5 square boxes you can view as a little
slide show: Cambridge, people on bicycles moving on a path; path
at the side of the square, woman in middle ground, grass, her arms
upraised to branch of tree, trunk at right-hand edge of square box,
bicycle with wicker basket leaning against trunk; foreground profile
of woman with shopping cart, young boy—son?—on her left side,
"moving" l. to r. across parking lot, or carpark, many cars lined up in
lot, at upper right, rear of man at open trunk, blue car; boats, water,
weeping willows.

lines up with collages, bcolly.jpg, torn lilies-of-the-valley, torn hibiscus,
white, red & pink, green and blue tears or tears; bcollx.jpg wooden
posts nailed to wood slats, blue, violet, cream & green, brown, pink;
polka dots, stripes, geometries, architectonics, an arm, a leg, a Bush in
the picture, history, climate, communities, societies, colors, patterns

"all bits of paper"
    Quote from Tom Raworth in Maggie O'Sullivan, "Dispatch from
                                                Marseilles,"
                         Chicago Review 48:4 Winter 2002/3

"Learn with the body."
    Yuasa Yasuo, *The Body: Toward an Eastern Mind-Body Theory.*
                  State University of New York, 1987

thrown into a (new) world
then affixed—here now, care for
the thing at hand, on hand, to hand
relieved of words in time and
sp(ace) but not for long

"all surfaces high-energy active"

                               Maggie O'Sullivan

"You must be your own severe critic by cutting and cutting at the words
until you get to what you need to say."
                Tom Raworth, Columbia College, Chicago

There is constant action and the action is in us.

"White dust was coming from the westbound tunnel."
                    Note from Ben, 11 July 2005
                            tomraworth.com

relief. devotion
and relief. from
come what may

a murmur of
some lost thrush
though I have never
seen one

                    Robert Creeley, "A Song"

syntax not chaos
disruption of the conventional
semantic elements into
"all bits of paper"

finite montages
put together
again, endlessly: The collages are quick and slow, fast to slow, seeing
them, looking at them, but once I slow down, can I speed up again?
Form is body including hands, the paper in hands, tearing or cutting
the paper in hand, placing the torn and cut paper, with glue, onto a
surface, I am looking at that surface with the glued torn and cut paper,
all form, me, they, he

picture a window
as we hear him
whistling softly

they flutter down but
then there's skin
on top or underneath
a hand, face among
draperies—the form
is possibility, that is,
form an extension of
content, that is, form
is impermanence, that
is form is not separate
that is form is
emptiness

"What I want is a kaleidoscope not a telescope."
                    Tom Raworth, *A Serial Biography*
                    Fulcrum Press, 1969

no preface to a picture
before thinking
thing becomes object
    the language
    pictures outside
   patience, patience
full of humility

"…the harbour silting up, rail tracks through the streets covered in
grass, empty steelworks."

              Ibid.

"It was a release to write it down."

              Ibid.

"those cheap paper pages with the fibres showing. The little squares
marked eggs; meat; cheese. Checked off each week with a long blue
tick. The sweet coupons you cut out, small as a postage stamp, and held
tight all the way to the shop."

              Ibid.

like autopoiesis, the pattern
remains although the entire
constitution is in flux
producing spectacle
making theatre
a universe of particulars

Ben's questions:
  "What's brown's second colour?"
  "What's mauve together?"

              Ibid.

order: an arrangement of objects
in lines or rows, forming grids

new order—musical composition,
painting, writing

"to give attention to similar
differences and different
similarities" says David Bohm in *Wholeness and the Implicate Order.*

His father "switches on the light and begins to read to (him) from
'What the Moon Saw,'" which I read too soon after, but it was called,
in the book I had, and still have, "A Picture Book Without Pictures,"
by Hans Christian Andersen. The telling that is the same form but is
different each night, a recursive panel for every night, thirty nights, 5 X
6 nights, a collage of collages.

"Let's jam the projector and let the beam burn a bright hole through
one still frame of time."

Tom Raworth, "Letters from Yaddo," *Visible Shivers*

All Fou*

corresponding reduplication
shift boundaries
bringing attention to form
within itself a multiple
continually traced
the lived all-at-once
"that arise and subside"
"in measurable time"

Francisco Varela, *Ethical Know-How*

distributed thinking
the unself, anemones,
"skillful means,
karuna—unconditional,
fearless, 'ruthless,' spontaneous
compassion" (Ibid)

"I really have no sense of questing for knowledge. At all. My idea is to
go the other way, you know. And to be completely empty and then see
what sounds."

Tom Raworth/Barry Alpert interview, *Vort 1* (Fall 1972)

---

*All Fou I happened to put a block of post-it notes down on a book on the table
beside me. me. I could see T.R.'s 4 X 4 collages and most of the title, but not the
'r' or the 's,' which gave me, among other things, *Amour fou* and the *Foo Fighters*.
At this point, I was reading (in *Removed for Further Study: The Poetry of Tom
Raworth, The Gig* 13/14) Ben Watson's "Tom Raworth, Gridlock Fragmentist: A
Poet Turns To Collage," the quotes from an interview done at T.R's. house where
he says (p.228): "I like the way the matte paper melds in with the Pritt to become
almost one surface." And on the facing page (p.229), "Every now and then I'm
happy to sit there and spend a long time with Pritt and paper." Pritt? Adhesive?
    If you Google Pritt, you see an anthropomorphic glue stick with a smiling
face, hands outstretched, showing a globe that has England, Europe, Asia &
Africa on the right, N. & S. America falling off on the left. Choose a country, it
said. Countries pop up. From Austria to the UK, no Africa, no America. Then
I noticed a kind of typewritten note at the bottom of the screen, "Note for US
Residents" and clicked on it. And got "This website is not intended for Residents
of the United States." What's up with *that*, I thought. "For US Residents, please
visit *www.henckel.us*." So I went there, and found, among others, the Pritt brand.
Dries clear and acid-free, archival safe, solvent-free and non-toxic. And part of
the Henckel Team, which has, on the US website, the logo of a duck. Duck
Products. On the right-hand side is a little box
                          (My plan is
                          these little boxes
                          make sequences…
                                    R. Creeley, *Pieces*)
like part of a Raworth collage. It had printed words and a drawing inside:
PERSONALS in a box, then SWM, HANDSOME, SEEKS DUCK TAPE
USER TO HELP ME OUT OF A STICKY SITUATION. DID I MENTION
THAT I'M HANDSOME? Drawing of squared-chinned white guy in cowboy-
type hat. In red, "click here" gets you to the Duck Tape Club Web Site and
Rock Tapewright (for that is his name) Adventure Contest. Wanna know more?
"Though not mentally strong, Rock Tapewright (you can click on his name)
possesses remarkable strength and courage, and a knack for getting into sticky

situations. Luckily, his faithful companion Major Stickwell (you can click on *his* name) is always at his side with a few words of wisdom and his trusty roll of Duck Tape." Click: Rock Tapewright: *occupation* man of adventure, *birthplace* Avon, OH, *interests* biochemistry, wrestling, *favorite color* blonde, etc. That's why Ohio is a red state. Whereas Major Stickwell, from Gloucestershire, England, and whose interest is translating ancient texts, whose fave color, or should I say colour, is beige, and whose favorite food is bangers and mash, takes us back to the world of Pritt, sold at Target and Wal-mart, for which I'd have to travel from San Francisco five miles and more, to Colma, Daly City, San Bruno, Albany, Oakland, El Cerrito, San Leandro—and more—to get it. And I'm sure I will, some day.

Raworth Day
Notre Dame University
20 September 2005

Published as a chapbook
Hooke Press
2006

Forever Amber

I heard a real poet* reading his work yesterday. Shattering. When I
looked at it in the book, I saw that there were no line breaks. Not
broken, shattered.
The sea captain tried to escape last night, but he was quickly captured
by the pirates
1) off the coast of Somalia
2) in the Gulf of Aden
Perfume overcomes the trigger, the trauma, the shattering.
dream➔Trauma
der Traum
As the man said, a little stimulation causes the line to break.
Wraps around
A tiny song:
Man with umbrella in backpack
So it won't rain
Nothing is reliable—look, my wrist doesn't move, the lines break, are
broken, no safety here/near (when my cane, its curve resting on the
table edge, falls down—crash—no one starts, stares. I pick it up
or will
)
Shooting schedule: shots of shots: e.g. 1-second shots of shooting
(guns) from familiar or unfamiliar western, adventure, period, dramatic,
comedy etc. movies
In blood we trust
uncertain ground➔coherence of vibration
travelers' reports➔disruption
other logics

Everything opens up. Pretending to read in order not to talk, moving
from thought to thought to thought. The line? What about it?
Your thoughts were elsewhere.
Why stop with one?
Have three.
(melt away)
I think I'll stop here
but then go on
read "beer and sun"

for "bees and sun"
jingle of a bell on a bike
thumbtack, its shadow on the wall
the shattering—hear it
?

*Raúl Zurita

A Broken Thing: Poets on the Line
ed. Rosko & Vander Zee
(University of Iowa Press—forthcoming 2011.)

Norma Cole is a poet, painter and translator. She teaches at the University of San Francisco. Cole has been the recipient of a Wallace Alexander Gerbode Foundation Award, Gertrude Stein Awards, an award from the Fund for Poetry, and an award from the Foundation for Contemporary Arts.

Photo Credit: Robert Eliason